The Classroom Management Survival Kit

Bulletin Boards, Student Activities and Teacher Ideas to Help You Motivate, Educate and Collaborate

by
Susanne Glover and Georgeann Grewe

illustrated by Georgeann Grewe

Cover by Janet Skiles

Copyright © 1994, Good Apple

ISBN No. 0-86653-782-1

Printing No. 9876

Good Apple
1204 Buchanan St., Box 299
Carthage, IL 62321-0299

Paramount Publishing

Dedication

In memory of Ron Paugh,
a fellow educator and former coauthor.
His humor will always remain with us.

GA1476

Table of Contents

GA1476

Introduction

You've taken the first step! You've purchased a book that will **motivate** teachers, students, and parents. Read Part I of *The Classroom Management Survival Kit* to find out how you can manage that eager group of children who enter your classroom!

Motivate yourself to present stimulating, developmentally appropriate lessons!

Motivate yourself to become more organized, both in preparing curriculum and in arranging your classroom!

Motivate students to learn by challenging their abilities, interests, and weaknesses!

Motivate parents to become involved in their children's education!

It's time to **educate** yourself. Turn the pages of this book to find a complete classroom resource book full of practical ideas, bulletin boards, activities, and programs to make your classroom management more effective! Part II will help you educate your students by implementing your individualized classroom management program.

Part III is designed to help school administrators, teachers, students, and parents **collaborate** on a comprehensive plan of behavior. Communication is the key to encouraging a positive relationship between home and school.

Motivate! **Educate**! **Collaborate**! Three simple steps for having the best teaching year ever!

GA1476

The Classroom Management Plan

This book is divided into three sections. Part I is designed to **motivate** teachers to plan and organize their classrooms. It will help teachers gain confidence in establishing their teaching and organizational skills. Read the ideas presented and adapt them to your classroom. Highlight teaching and management suggestions for future reference. Write in your own ideas to personalize this plan.

Part II is designed to **educate** teachers. There are nine bulletin boards, one for each school month beginning in September and ending in May. The bulletin boards are the visual summary of the classroom behavior you are targeting for a particular month (or other time period). For each bulletin board you will find patterns and design suggestions; a weekly behavior chart; a conduct card; a letter from the teacher to be sent home explaining the targeted behavior and the conduct grade; a form for student letters to be sent home; station or cooperative learning ideas; and finally, ways to "celebrate" good behavior with your students.

Part III is your written behavioral management system. It is designed to be photocopied and kept in a large, three-ring notebook. You will find all of the necessary forms to place in this notebook. Use the behavior lists provided to schedule when certain behavior will be taught. Collect conduct cards in individual conduct card envelopes. Place current and used behavior charts in your notebook for reference. This notebook will contain your evaluation system. Refer to it often as you teach behavior, review it, and plan new behavior to target. At your fingertips will be a comprehensive notebook which will enable you to **collaborate** with administrators, teachers, parents, and students.

The following page will give you thorough, step-by-step directions for organizing, implementing, and evaluating your classroom management program!

GA1476

Organizing the Plan

It's time to set up your program. Just follow these simple steps using the month of September as a guide.

1. Buy a large three-ring notebook. Copy these pages to insert in your notebook: 132, 133, 134, 44, 135, 136, 137, 138, 139, 140.
   a. Use page 132 as the first notebook page. Fill in your name, school, and grade.
   b. Use page 133, the Table of Contents, for your second page. This will be the checklist of items needed for the notebook and the order in which they are to be placed in the notebook. Add additional items to this list as you feel necessary, being sure to mark them on the Table of Contents page.
   c. Make enough copies of the Emergency Form on page 134 for each child in your class (and a few extra). Ask families to fill it out and return it to school as soon as possible. Be sure that all information is accurate. You will want to keep it updated throughout the year. If your school already has an emergency form, you may use that form instead. (A second copy of each form could be kept in the school office for quick reference.)
   d. Make two copies of the September Behavior Chart found on page 44. List the names of each student in your class alphabetically. (Now copy this chart four more times so that your class names are already written and your charts will last you through the month of September.)
   e. Copy pages 135, 136, 137, and 138 to use as your Behavior Checklist. This will help you to plan your behavior program for the year.
   f. Get enough clasp envelopes ($6^1/2$" x $9^1/2$" [16.49 x 24.11 cm] or larger) for each child in your class. Copy page 139 so that you can glue the form on the front of each envelope. You will collect conduct cards in these throughout the entire year. Keep good records so that you can readily see whether or not a child has returned a signed conduct card each month.
   g. As your final notebook sheet, make several copies of page 140. This form will make it simple for you to record phone calls, family conferences, notes home, etc., and the dates they occurred. (You might want to insert a large clasp envelope punched with three holes in which to place notes.)

Now that you have organized your notebook, the fun begins.

2. Select a bulletin board. (We will use the mouse idea for September found on page 41.) Enlarge the mouse pattern on page 42 and copy several apple patterns (page 43). (You may want to laminate the patterns before you place them on the bulletin board.)

3. Make a few blank signs for behavior. Each sign represents one type of behavior you will target for the month. For a list of possible behaviors, see pages 135-138. Look over the list and decide which behaviors you would like to address during the month of September. Select a title for your bulletin board appropriate for the behavior you choose to target. (We will use **Quiet as a Mouse**.) During the first week we will stress the behavior **line up quietly**. Write this on your first sign to display under Behavior on the bulletin board. Record this behavior on your Classroom Behavior Chart on page 44 in your three-ring notebook, being sure to write in the dates it will be taught. Each time a child misbehaves, cross out an apple by his name on the behavior chart for that day of the week.

4. Determine your class goal. (Let's say you have twenty-five students.) Your goal for the week might be five apples to place on the bulletin board, one for each day of the week. To earn an apple each day, suppose that you want eighteen out of twenty-five children to have **no** apples crossed out on their behavior charts for that particular day. When that goal of eighteen or more per day has been met, then place one apple on the bulletin board. You as a teacher must determine how many children daily can achieve good behavior for lining up quietly. (Make it simple enough for children to achieve success, but challenging enough that good behavior is demanded.) At the end of the week, review the skill of lining up quietly with your students. If behavior is acceptable, select another behavior for the following week. If you find that children still need to work on lining up quietly, try it for another week, or choose another behavior and work on lining up quietly later in the year.

At the beginning of week number two, place another desired behavior on your bulletin board. (This time we'll try **face the front** when lining up.) Use the same procedure as week number one. Set a goal and try to reach it. Go to your classroom notebook and list the behavior at the top of your behavior chart. Record it on your list of behaviors, pages 135-138. Continue these procedures for the month of September. Always examine your goals daily and discuss them with your class. Be positive whenever possible. Talk about negative behavior and ways to make it better.

5. At the end of the month, examine the behavior charts. Do you see good progress? Are the same students the ones having difficulty? What will you do about it?

6. Make a mouse conduct card for each student. (See page 45 for the pattern.) As your students work on behavior during the month of September, determine how you will establish satisfactory or unsatisfactory grades. (How many "bad" apples did the child earn?) Check the behavior chart for each child. Let's say that Josh had three apples crossed out during the entire month, two the first week and one the second, for a total of three "bad" apples. Punch three apples from the twenty on his conduct card. Both you and the parents can readily see how Josh is doing. Be patient. This program may take a little while to establish, but it will be worthwhile to everyone involved. At the end of September, record the grade on the conduct card and send it home to be reviewed and signed by a family member. Have children return the signed cards to school to be placed in the child's individual conduct card envelope. Record "returned" or "not returned" on the outside form on each envelope for quick reference.

7. Inform families of your classroom management plan by sending home the letter from the teacher on page 46 which indicates the behavior that you targeted during September and how your grading system works. This letter should accompany the child's conduct card. Also have the children write letters home using the form on page 47. In this way, children assess how they behaved during the month as they write home. (You may need to give your children a few ideas to get them started.) They may want to color the picture on their letter home. If negative behavior warrants a parent conference, call the parents to set this up if they do not contact you first. Be sure to record this type of communication on the form (page 140) which you will have placed in your management notebook.

8. Now is the time to review the behavior that you targeted during the month of September (**line up quietly; face the front; walk properly**.) Discuss positive and negative results with your students. Be sure to praise good behavior. Reschedule behavior that needs to be practiced again during the school year. Be sure to keep your list of behaviors (pages 135-138) up to date. After you have reviewed your September behavior, it's time to begin again.

9. Look ahead to the month of October. Start with step 1 and begin organizing your notebook, bulletin board, etc. Observe your class carefully and see what behavior should be targeted next. Go for it!

   ** Use family helpers or classroom aids to help you in organizing the information, forms, cards, letters, etc. Plan wisely and be consistent.

   ** Some bulletin boards are seasonal and relate to a particular month. Others may be adapted. Be sure to supplement with additional bulletin boards for June, July, August, or any month you may wish to change.

GA1476

A Taste of Whole Language

One of the many features of this book is that it provides the teacher with ideas, activities, and resources to integrate classroom learning. During the month of September (as with most months) we encourage you to plan independent, small, and large group activities with your class. The apple scavenger hunt is an example of a cooperative learning activity. It is important that you **teach** children to cooperate as group members. Children will not already know how to do this. They must be taught and retaught. **Practice** with them and give them lots of opportunities to work in different types of groups. One way of establishing cooperative learning groups is described on page 87. This is only one example. There are many. Read about them. Invent your own, but always allow children time to experiment. Both you and your class will want to assess often. Monitor groups closely and spend time sharing comments, both positive and negative. Some months have station ideas suggested. Implement them whenever possible. Children will enjoy working independently and sharing with the class.

Another feature of this book is a culminating activity page (see the September Celebrate on page 48). Use these ideas to reward your class for good behavior. Use one or all of the suggestions. Try using one each week, or simply take time at the end of the month to **celebrate**!

Display the behavior poems (see pages 7-24) in strategic places in your classroom to promote positive reminders about behavior. Teach the songs suggested. For targeting the September behavior of **lining up**, select poems and songs from pages 12, 13, and 19. The children will love them. (Use them for handwriting practice, choral reading, for memorizing, or just plain fun!)

GA1476

POEMS and SONGS

Motivate your students with these poems and songs. Display them in your classroom for reminders about good behavior. Memorize the poems to recite to other children. Practice the poems for choral readings. Copy the songs in your best handwriting to display around the school. Have a sing-along and entertain other classes!

7

GA1476

My Classroom

My classroom is a special place
    Where I can feel at ease;
I have a tidy little desk
    Beneath the window's breeze.

The chalkboard's way up in the front,
    The bookshelves line the wall;
My teacher's desk is near the door
    So she can see the hall.

The classroom's really colorful,
    With decorations bright;
My friends and I have made them—
    We think they look just right!

Our stories are published everywhere
    For everyone to read;
Green plants are hanging all around,
    And we've got fish to feed.

My teacher makes it fun to learn,
    About almost anything;
We laugh and think and play and write
    We put on plays and sing.

My teacher gives us jobs to do,
    We always do our share;
We wash the boards, and we pick up trash,
    It seems that we all care.

Our class has got school spirit,
    And it's something we can't hide;
For when we talk about our school
    Our hearts are full of pride!

GA1476

Oops!

The alarm went off this morning
But I was still half asleep,
So I pulled up all my covers,
And I didn't make a peep.
I dreamed that I was at the beach
Just playing in the sand,
And then I waded out in the surf
Where I could hardly stand.
The waves began to pull me
Where the water was too deep,
I shook and then I shivered.
Where was I? Asleep?
The clock said it was nearly eight;
I put on my shirt and jeans,
I gobbled down some breakfast—
Cold hot dogs and pork-n-beans.
I hurried to the corner
Just as the school bus stopped,
I jumped right on and found a seat,
Beside my friend I flopped.
It seemed just minutes later,
That the bus doors opened wide.
I hurried up the steps at school
And found my place inside.
Oops! I forgot my backpack,
With all my school supplies,
Sitting on my bus seat—
I felt my panic rise.
My lunch—I'd left it in the fridge,
My homework—(What was it?)
By now it didn't matter,
Not even just a bit!
I wish this hadn't happened.
It wasn't meant to be.
I wish, I wish, I wish, I wish
That today was Saturday!

GA1476

Be Prepared

Every day when I go to school
    I check in my backpack,
To see that I remembered
    What I needed to bring back—
Homework, pencils, paper, lunch,
    And most importantly,
The books for all my classes,
    Work my parents had to see.
My notes are signed, my work is neat,
    I've checked it once or twice;
My day begins 'cause I'm prepared,
    The feeling's rather nice!

Assemblies

Assemblies can be lots of fun
    If we each do our part;
So quietly we gather,
    And wait for them to start.
The speakers, then, are introduced,
    Just what fun lies ahead?
We'll listen very carefully
    To everything that's said.
There's always something to be learned—
    New thoughts, ideas to share;
Information, entertainment,
    Advice from those who care.
When the programs are over,
    And we go our separate ways,
Remember those assemblies,
    That brightened up our days.

GA1476

Staying in My Seat

My teacher will know
    When he looks in my chair,
I'll be busily working
    And staying right there.
I will not get up
    'Till he says that I may;
I'll remember to stay
    In my seat every day.

My Seat

My teacher assigns us each a seat
    To call our very own;
It's here that we do lots of things
    Sitting quietly, working alone.

Once in awhile we can move our chairs,
    Into circles or groups they go;
But my favorite place that is home to me
    Is my chair at the end of the row.

Sometimes when I work it is hard to sit still
    So I fidget and wiggle around;
I invent ways to sit with my legs under me
    And I try not to make even a sound.

Lining Up

I will not shove, I will not push,
    I will not try to pass;
I will not lag behind the rest,
    I'll line up with my class!

GA1476

Walking in Line

There is a trick to walking in line,
    Especially when I'm in the front;
It seems that all of the kids behind me
    Are involved in various stunts.
There is a trick to walking in line,
    Especially when I'm in the middle;
It seems that all the kids who surround me,
    All like to stop and fiddle.
There is a trick to walking in line,
    Especially when I'm in the back;
The children all bunch together up front,
    It seems that they've lost the knack
Of walking in line, making one straight row,
    That stretches with all of us in it;
To and from classes, and out in the halls,
    Can we keep it this way—for a minute?
There is a trick to walking in line,
    If you listen and do as you're asked,
Keep your eyes to the front and your hands to yourself
    And you'll move right along to your task.

Attention

Our line stays perfectly straight,
As long as we don't have to wait;
We'll get where we're going,
Then we can start doing
What we need to and we won't be late!

GA1476

Being Last in Line

The kids all push to be first in line
But little do they know,
My favorite spot is the last one in line
Where no one else wants to go.

I walk along slowly and look at the sky,
I see shadows that fall on the ground;
I notice the cracks in the sidewalk,
And autumn leaves tumbling down.

I find it so peaceful, with no bouncy footsteps
To land on the top of my shoe;
Go ahead, get in line, hurry up to the front
So that I can be last—behind you!

Manners

My family always taught me
   What to say and what to do,
So I could handle anything
   And proudly make it through.
Casually or formally,
   With friends or grown-ups, too,
I know when it's appropriate
   To say "Please" and "Thank you."

GA1476

The Library

The library is my favorite place,
　　It always seems so bright;
The room is full of quiet,
　　The books are my delight.

I love to study all the new books,
　　Lined up on the shelf;
So carefully I must decide
　　Which ones I can read by myself.

I make sure that my hands are clean,
　　Before I touch any books;
Then carefully I open them
　　To get a better look.

The print is right, the pictures really
　　Make books so inviting;
I can't wait until I can read
　　This book—think how exciting!

I'll let the thoughts fill up my head,
　　I'll learn new things, you'll see—
The library is a wonderful place,
　　For friends like us to be!

Following Directions

My teacher's here to guide me,
She will tell me what to do;
She will give me good directions.
I will listen. How about you?

Listening

LOOK! LOOK! LISTEN! LISTEN!
So you'll not be the one who's missin'
Out on work; out on fun;
LISTEN! LISTEN! Everyone!

Chatter

The kids were all talking at me.
Whose voice it was I couldn't see.
There was so much chatter
And that was the matter,
That wasn't the way it should be!

Then slowly I looked in their eyes.
And they knew that look—no disguise!
Hands went into the air,
I called each one with care.
Now each voice could be heard—no surprise!

GA1476

Raise Your Hand

"If you have news to share,"
    said my teacher one day,
"Please raise your hand
    and we'll hear what you say.
I will call you by name
    and our class will all show
That it's your turn to talk.
    Please tell us what you know.
Face the class and speak clearly,
    so that we may all hear
Your response, your opinions,
    or thoughts you hold dear."

Patience

My teacher asked a question
    and I gave it lots of thought;
Then I slowly raised my hand
    to do just as I'd been taught.
Then someone yelled the answer out,
    and I felt aggravated;
I wished that he had raised his hand
    like me—I patiently waited!

Taking Turns

Sometimes it's hard to wait my turn
    for I get so excited;
Often the words just blurt right out.
    They haven't been invited.
I must remember to wait until
    my teacher calls on me.
I'll raise my hand and quietly wait—
    that's how it has to be!

GA1476

Fire Drills

The room was full of quiet,
    Thoughts were spinning in my head;
I was concentrating deeply
    About the things my teacher said.

Then I heard the sudden buzzer
    As the fire alarm did sound;
I jumped up, quickly walked outside,
    My eyes glanced all around.

My class had gone out single file,
    No noises did we make;
We lined up at our "meeting spot"
    Just minutes did this take!

We counted heads and stood real still,
    The teacher called our names;
In silence we all waited
    Until the signal came.

Bathroom Break

When I go to the bathroom
    I must hurry on my way;
I'll ask before I leave the room,
    I will not stop and play.
I'll flush the toilet when I'm through,
    I'll wash and dry my hands;
And then I'll walk straight back to class
    As quickly as I can.

GA1476

The Lunchroom

My stomach's growling, has been growling,
    All I want is food . . . .
Pizza, hot dogs, salad bar,
    Will get me in the mood.
Will it be soup or saucy spaghetti,
    Or peanut butter and jelly?
Food, food, just give me food,
    Wonderful, hot and smelly . . ..
I've been standing in the lunchroom line,
    My stomach's growling still,
I cannot wait to get my food,
    So I can eat my fill.
Fill up that plate, up to the top,
    With veggies, fruit, and meat;
Please don't forget that I'm a kid
    And I need lots to eat.
      I'll drink my milk and clean my plate,
        And mind my manners, too!
      For this is the part of the day that I like
        When I eat with friends like you!

Advice

My dad tells me to work real hard
And make good grades in school;
My mom tells me to listen
And to follow every rule;
My grandpa says to eat my lunch
And play outside each day;
My grandma says to be a friend
To those I meet today;
My sister says to do my homework
On time, and never be late;
My brother says to study well
So I can graduate;
As for myself, what shall it be?
I'll do it all and be PROUD of ME!

GA1476

School Spirit

(Sing to the tune of "Jingle Bells")

Verse:
It's off to school we go
So early in the day,
In rain or snow or shine,
We hurry on our way.
Hear the school bells ring,
Ringing loud and clear,
What fun it is to work and play
And learn throughout the year.

Chorus:
Working, playing, singing, laughing,
Sharing with a friend;
Oh what fun we have at school
From morning 'till the end.
Working, playing, singing, laughing,
Sharing with a friend;
Oh what fun we have at school
From morning 'till the end.

Lining Up

(Sing to the tune of "Oh Susanna")

Every time that I must get in line,
    I stand so straight and tall;
I keep my arms down by my side,
    I do not move at all.

My head is facing forward,
    My eyes look straight ahead;
My lips are closed, my ears are open,
    Listening to what's said.

GA1476

Good Manners

(Sing to the tune of "She'll Be Comin' 'Round the Mountain")

I'll remember to say "Please" when I should,
I'll remember to say "Please" when I should,
I will try to be polite,
Every morning, noon and night,
I'll remember to say "Please" when I should.

I'll remember to say "Thank you" when I should,
I'll remember to say "Thank you" when I should,
I will try to be polite,
Every morning, noon and night,
I'll remember to say "Thank you" when I should.

I'll remember to say "May I" when I should,
I'll remember to say "May I" when I should,
I will try to be polite,
Every morning, noon and night,
I'll remember to say "May I" when I should.

I'll remember to say "Excuse me" when I should,
I'll remember to say "Excuse me" when I should,
I will try to be polite,
Every morning, noon and night,
I'll remember to say "Excuse me" when I should.

I will try to be polite in every way,
I will watch what things I do and what I say,
"Please" and "Thank you" you will hear,
"Excuse me, may I, Mother dear,"
I will try to be polite in every way.

In the Library

(Sing to the tune of "Eensy, Weensy Spider")

I went into the library
    and all was quiet there.
I found a super book to read,
    I checked it out with care.
I read all of the pages
    and I needed a new book.
So I went back to the library
    to take another look!

Are You Listening

(Sing to the tune of "Frere Jacques")

Are you listening, are you listening,
Everyone, Everyone.
Listen to what I say. Listen to what I say.
Then have fun. Then have fun.

*Try this song in a round!

GA1476

If You're Following Directions

(Sing to the tune of "If You're Happy and You Know It")

If you're following directions, *wink your eye*,
If you're following directions, *wink your eye*,
If you know just what to do,
Then give me your little clue,
If you're following directions, *wink your eye*.

Additional verses:
Sing as above but use these directions:
2. nod your head;
3. stand up straight;
4. tap your toe;
5. raise your hand;
6. smile at me;
7. wave hello;
(Add extra verses that you or your class might create!)

Following Directions

(Sing to the tune of "Yellow Rose of Texas")

I will listen to my teacher,
 I will do as I am told;
I will follow all directions—
 When I'm young and when I'm old.

Good directions are important,
 I must listen, think, and do
All those little tasks they ask me.
 Step by step I'll make it through.

Fire Drill

(Sing to the tune of "The Ants Go Marching")

Whenever we have a fire drill we walk, we walk;
Whenever we have a fire drill we walk, we walk;
We walk in a straight line and out the door,
We never know what the emergency's for
So we quickly, quietly, hurry outside to wait.

Whenever we have a fire drill don't talk, don't talk;
Whenever we have a fire drill don't talk, don't talk;
We walk with our lips closed and stand in line.
Our teachers will tell us when all is fine,
So we quietly, patiently, stand in a line and wait.

Whenever we have a fire drill we stand, we stand;
Whenever we have a fire drill we stand, we stand;
We stand in a line with our eyes straight ahead,
We want to be list'ning to what is said
So we all can quickly, safely return to class.

Eat Your Food

(Sing to the tune of "Row, Row, Row Your Boat")

Carefully select your food,
Then eat what's on your tray;
Cut it up, chew it up, 'till it's gone,
Let's eat right every day.

GA1476

Recess

(Sing to the tune of "London Bridge")

We are going outside to play, out to play,
   out to play.
We are going outside to play.
We'll go safely.

We will watch where we are going, we are going,
   we are going.
We will watch where we are going.
We'll walk safely.

We will climb and run with care, run with care,
   run with care.
We will climb and run with care.
We'll play safely.

Make New Friends

Make new friends
   but keep the old;
One is silver
   and the other gold.

*Try this song in a round!

GA1476

Arranging Your Room

Many discipline problems can be prevented by thinking through the physical arrangement of your classroom. Both adults and children need their own space.

Look at the furniture and the physical structure of your room. Be sure to keep fire exits, doors, and main traffic patterns open. Know where you will place large and/or heavy pieces of furniture. Don't block built-in cupboards, drawers, closets, shelves, or other valuable storage units.

You will want an area for your desk, filing cabinet, teaching supplies, manuals, etc., that will not obstruct the view of the chalkboard. Make yourself a little corner so that all materials are tidy and easily accessible to you.

Now look at seating for the children. Do you have individual desks that can be moved? Do children work at tables? Do you want desks/tables separated? Do you want small and large group spaces available?

Think about your teaching style. Do you enjoy having children sit on the floor around you? Do you need a chalkboard nearby? Provide a space large enough to seat your entire class where furniture won't have to be moved. Use this space for story time, calendar/circle time, guest speakers, demonstrations, audiovisuals, etc. Provide an area for group work, either using table or floor space. Do you have reference books placed where children can use them easily? Will you need a quiet corner? Do you want a time-out area where children can think about problems? Is space available for station work?

When children are seated facing one another, expect more communication. This is great for teamwork and cooperative learning activities, but it may encourage too much socializing. Isolating children in individual seats discourages teamwork and may encourage children to become more dependent upon the teacher. Arranging students in pairs facing the teacher allows for peer tutoring and some teamwork. Seating possibilities are numerous, with both positive and negative aspects. You must decide which arrangement will provide the most peaceful and productive classroom atmosphere. Keep it simple, creative, and positive!

GA1476

Getting Organized

Being organized will save you lots of time. Not only will you find it easier to plan and carry out activities, but you will be a wonderful example to your students. If you are organized, there will be less time for children to wander off task and become discipline problems. Organizational skills need to be taught and practiced!

Many supplies in your room will be off-limits to children. Let them know what personal properties are yours! Label them if you need to. Use your storage space wisely for materials your students may use. Label these and expect that your borrowed materials be respected and returned to their proper place immediately after use. (You may want a few persons in the room to be in charge of the supplies cupboard, rather than several children getting into materials.) Small, vinyl, two-divider cleaning trays with handles are ideal. Place scissors, rulers, a few boxes of crayons, etc., in each one. Place these on each table, at stations, or in the supplies cupboard to be used when needed. Tie yarn onto scissors and label supplies with your name so that classroom supplies can be easily identified.

Many storage containers and art supplies come directly from the grocery store. Pringles™ cans, Styrofoam™ trays and cups, cardboard produce baskets, twist ties, butter tubs, squeeze bottles, egg cartons, boxes, bags, plastic jars, and bottles are just a few practical examples of items to use for storage or as project builders. It is essential that when you collect items, you remember where you put them. Make a list and write the items inventoried on the outside of your drawer, file cabinet, or art cupboard! Creative time will be an opportunity for fun, rather than a stressful time when both teacher and class are trying to get all materials together for a project. Store manipulatives in the same way. You'll enjoy using them more often if they are at your fingertips!

Be sure that a special place (inside or outside the classroom) is reserved for coats, hats, lunch boxes, and book bags. Be sure that students label their belongings. Children want their own property respected too!

GA1476

Classroom Procedures for You and Your Substitute

Establishing procedures in your classroom on the first day of school will get your class started on the right foot. Let students know exactly what you expect for each procedure, and be consistent in following through. After the first week, constantly evaluate and review the procedures with your class. Remember to praise your students for a job well done. Children like order. They like schedules. They like to know the plan. Let them know what is happening that might deviate from the daily routine. Then you will not be frustrated by repeating the agenda, and students will not be kept in suspense!

Here is a checklist of procedures you need to establish during the first week of school. Make a copy for your substitute teacher file.

_____What is the class schedule

_____Where to put coats, hats, lunches, book bags

_____Where to put my books/extra supplies

_____Where to sit

_____Where to line up

_____How to line up

_____What class signals are used (bells, lights, whistles, hand signals)

_____Where to stack chairs

_____Where to find lunch tickets

_____Where to put completed work/homework

GA1476

_____Where to find makeup work

_____Who does what job

_____Who is the teacher's helper

_____What does the teacher's helper do

_____When to go to the bathroom

_____When to get drinks

_____What are the lunchroom rules

_____What are the playground rules

_____What are the bathroom rules

_____Where to go for morning bus

_____Where to go for evening bus

_____Where is the lost and found

_____What is my class number/how is it used

_____Where are classroom supplies

_____How to change classes

Points to Ponder

- Be positive with your students. Look at the bright side, especially when helping children with difficulties. Find something in a child worth complimenting. It will promote good self-esteem.

- Encourage children to plan with you. They will become more excited and motivated by doing something they choose to do.

- Have children line up by number, ABC order, or in some designated way. When student #1 has had a turn lining up first for the day, have him or her move to the back of the line so that student #2 can be first the next day, and so on. In this way, every child will get a day to be first in line. If you have behavior problems following one of the above suggestions, simply move the problem child to another designated spot and continue the rotation.

- Give oral directions to your students only when children have eye contact with you. Keep your directions short and clear. Write the directions/page numbers on the chalkboard as a reminder of the assignment. When you finish giving directions, ask a child to repeat them back to the class.

- Seat children with learning problems nearest the chalkboard or teaching area. Seat shorter children near the front of the room so they can see easily.

- Seat your children beside different classmates throughout the year. Explain to your students how important it is to be able to get along with many different types of people.

- Teach your children how to work in groups. This skill must be taught! Begin with students working in pairs. Provide numerous opportunities for children to do this. Expect each child in the pair to be responsible for something. After lots of practice, children can begin to work in groups of three or four students. Read books about cooperative learning to find out strategies that you might want to try.

GA1476

- Repeat directions only once or twice to your students to encourage them to listen. You don't want to find yourself repeating directions several times.

- Expect a lot from your class. The more you expect of them, the more they will give you!

- Be prepared for those "in-between" moments when children are waiting for something, when schedules suddenly change, for emergencies, for rainy days. Enjoy these ongoing activities with your students:
  1. Read a chapter book, poetry book, or book of short stories.
  2. Plan a mural. It could be seasonal or content related. Hang it on a wall so children work on it without disturbing others.
  3. Set up a table in your room where children can work a jigsaw puzzle. Leave the puzzle there so they can work on it during free time.
  4. Decide on a class project. Place the materials in a corner of the room where students can work.
  5. Start a question jar. Provide small cards on which questions can be written by you or other children. Be sure to include all content areas. Place questions in the jar. See which student can be your class "expert" and answer the most!
  6. Have each child keep a journal. Assign topics about things studied, stories read, activities. Be sure to allow time for journal writing to be shared with the class!
  7. Set up a "mailbox" in your classroom. Encourage children to write letters, postcards, etc., to others in the class. Ask your teacher's helper for the day to be messenger and deliver the mail.
  8. Play the game Simon Says. Children love the challenge and you will be amazed at what good listeners you will develop.

GA1476

9. Write creative dramatic ideas on individual cards and place them in a container. Children love seasonal ideas. Have children select a card and act it out for the class to guess.
10. Enjoy a "fitness break" by leading the class in simple exercises. They'll enjoy the stretch!
11. Have children clean their desks, bookshelves, etc.
12. Play a memory game.
13. Ask children to do mental math with you. Choose skills appropriate to your grade level.
14. Use a large map that children can see and play a geography game by having children see who can find a particular place first.

- Get your class excited about reading by selecting special books that have a "catchy" gimmick to them. Examples: mirrors; search for Santa/Waldo; clues (*The Eleventh Hour* by Graeme Base. New York: Harry N. Abrams, Inc., 1989). Look for books with special types of art/illustrations.

- Speak softly to your students. This will encourage them to listen carefully.

- Make positive phone calls home. Ask your "star" student to listen on the other phone as the family receives the call.

- Have children create your bulletin boards. Give them ideas, if necessary. Provide materials. Give students ample time to complete them. Set deadlines.

- Begin a class newspaper. This will provide a great experience for all children to become involved in some way. Students will love reading about themselves and their class. What skills the children will exercise with this project!

Do You Need a Job Chart?

Busy hands and many volunteers to help may be a sign that you need to organize a job chart in your classroom. Depending upon the age and composition of your class, you may find that your children are multi-talented and enjoy helping you constantly. To avoid conflicts and confusion, determine what chores need to be done and how often. Post the jobs and who is responsible for completing them.

Sometimes it is a good idea to survey the talents in your room. Ask children to write brief summaries of what they do best. Create job charts from the interests of the children.

Another option is to compile a list of numerous chores you find that are important in your classroom. Such a list might include:

1. Board Washer—cleans boards, dusts erasers, puts out new chalk
2. Secretary—writes invitations, thank-yous, etc.
3. Greeter—meets visitors and is their host
4. Green Thumb Expert—waters plants
5. Veterinarian—cares for class pets
6. Art Supplies Director—passes out/collects art supplies
7. Floor Supervisor—straightens desks/cleans floor
8. Energy Saver—opens and closes windows when asked/turns lights on and off when necessary
9. Audiovisual Manager—knows how to properly run/care for equipment
10. Coat Supervisor—makes sure clothing/book bags are cared for properly and taken home each day
11. Errand Boy/Girl—(always two children) to carry messages
12. Equipment Manager—carries playground equipment
13. Room Monitor—makes sure all books/materials are in their proper places and organized

Decide if certain children will be responsible for one task all year or if you will rotate jobs. Usually weekly job assignments work best. Teach your children to become responsible members of the class. It will be a great year!

GA1476

Teacher's Helper

There are many ways to solve the problem of too many volunteers for the job. Consider choosing one child to be your helper for the day. Often the jobs you have require only one (or two) sets of extra hands and very little time. By focusing on one child per day, each student may feel elated to be the one who gets to do everything. By the same token, though, all responsibility for the job falls on that child. He or she learns both the pleasures and duties of being the teacher's helper.

Pleasure: (you may choose all or several for the teacher's helper)
1. Provide a special desk at which the child may work.
2. Allow the child to write in pen.
3. Allow the child to do classwork on the chalkboard.
4. Allow the child to help other children having difficulty (provided he or she has the skills to do this).
5. Let the child be first in all activities.
6. Allow the child to sit by a friend for classwork and/or during lunch.

Duties:
1. Pass out and collect all papers for the day (work sheets, notes home, homework, classwork).
2. Wash the chalkboard and dust erasers.
3. Distribute art supplies and other necessary materials and collect them.
4. Run errands (take lunch count, absences to office).
5. Record homework and gather books, materials, etc., for children who are absent.
6. Host guest speakers (eat lunch with them, show them around the school).
7. Be a "buddy" to new children who enter the class.
8. Ask the child to get equipment, show filmstrips, etc.
9. Have the child be line leader.

GA1476

Build a Better Classroom Through Incentive Projects

Here are some great ways to inspire children to behave well. Good behavior can be rewarding both for you and your students. Good things will happen as a result of a team approach to appropriate discipline.

Explain to your school administration the incentive project idea explained below. He or she may also suggest that your class be allowed to raise money to begin the program. He or she may also suggest that you check with the PTO or other parent organization to help with funding. Consider, too, families of your students, residents in the community, or business partners in education to support you financially, materially, or with expertise. Although money is often a major factor, some projects suggested below require only hard work on the part of you and your students. Present all or several ideas listed below to your class. These are merely suggestions. You may wish to provide additional ideas that are more meaningful to your grade level.

This is how the program works. Children can earn points for good behavior. Pretend that your class decides they would like to go on a field trip as a reward. Let's say it will take 100 points to go on the field trip. (This point system will have to be determined by you and your individual class to make it appropriate. This is just an example.) Pretend that your class has been working on the behavior "lining up." Each time that your class is asked to line up (after you have explained to them how this is to be done), they can earn one point if the majority of the children lined up properly. Children line up several times during the day, so it may be possible to earn ten points per day. As you accumulate points, children will need a visible reminder of their success. Use a wall chart, tickets in a container on your desk, a bulletin board, a graph, etc., to record progress. Each time you reach a mini goal, let's say ten points, complete a part of your plan.

GA1476

This is how it might be organized:

Reward: Field Trip

10 points —Decide on location (zoo).

20 points —Review zoo brochures to determine details about your trip (reservations, dates, times, costs, transportation, chaperones, lunch, etc.).

30 points —Determine the cost of the trip and how you will pay for it.

40 points —Make tentative reservations at the zoo; check with your principal about transportation (bus, car, foot, etc.).

50 points —Reserve buses; create a field trip form (you may want to use the one in this book on page 39). If going by car, determine the number of cars or vans needed.

60 points —Contact chaperones to assist on the trip.

70 points —Plan the trip itinerary.

80 points —Send home field trip permission forms.

90 points —Contact the zoo, bus drivers, family chaperones to confirm the field trip schedule.

100 points —Congratulations! Have fun on your trip!

It is hoped that children will see the rewards of their efforts for good behavior. And think of all they have learned along the way! Each step of the reward required responsibility on the part of each student in planning and discussing the field trip. How much more meaningful it should be for the children to know that they were involved from the beginning. Success for each child meant success for the group. Isn't that what teaching and learning are all about: "We are all in this together!"

GA1476

Here is a list of **classroom projects** you and your children may want to consider. Don't let this list limit you! You and your class can be most creative and stir up a little fun yourselves! (After each idea, you will find several words listed to help you establish your point system as shown in the example on the previous page.)

1. Build an aquarium—tank, filter, gravel, pump, fish food, fish, plants, hood, aquarium stand, books.

2. Build a terrarium—tank or glass container, rocks, plants, potting soil, lamp, water/food containers, books, food, animals (optional).

3. Build an ant farm—ant farm, sand, ants, books about ants.

4. Library—shelves, library card pockets, date due slips, date/stamp pad, books, file card box, book ends.

5. Field trips—see previous page.

6. Guest speakers—topics of interest, calendar dates, money for honorarium (plane ticket, lodging, meals, transportation to and from presentation, hosts, equipment the speaker may need, letters of invitation, thank-yous.

7. Playground—repair old equipment, purchase new equipment, paint, landscaping, mulch, grass seed, benches, picnic table, trees.

8. Picnic area—picnic tables, paint, benches, trees, mulch, tablecloth.

9. Activity center—tables, chairs, computer, software, games, partitions, part-time aid or parent helper, art supplies, (equipment geared for any specific type of center you might wish to create).

10. Quilt—fabric, quilting books, sewing machine, quilting frames, straight pins, fabric scissors, quilt binding, quilt batting, quilting thread, fabric crayons or markers, marking pens for fabric, table.

11. Class album—camera, film, photo albums, labels, fine-point permanent markers, money to develop film.

12. Class newspaper—table, typewriter or computer, typing paper, photocopy machine, camera, film, money to develop film, stapler, staples.

13. Adopt a nursing home—stationery, stamps, pens, names and addresses of patients, art supplies, family helpers (for transportation of children or delivery of projects).

14. _____ —

15. _____ —

16. _____ —

GA1476

Homework

_____   _____
(Child's Name)   (Date)

Class	Textbook	Workbook	Other
Reading			
Spelling			
Math			
Writing			
Science			
Social Studies			
Health			
Language			
Music			
Art			
Media			
Phys. Ed.			
Other			

_____
(Parent/Guardian Signature)   (Date)

Class Field Trip

Name of Activity:_____

_____

Where: _____

When: _____

Time: _____

How: (a) on foot   (b) by car   (c) by bus   (d) other

Why: _____

_____

_____

Cost: _____

(Please send the money to school with your child's permission slip.)

Teacher/s in charge: _____

- -

Please return this section to school with your child.

(Child's name)_____

has my permission to attend (activity) _____

_____

on (date) _____

I understand that he/she will be traveling by _____

and that the cost of the trip will be_____

(Family signature) _____

(Family phone number) _____

_____ My child may **not** attend. My child will **not** attend school that day.

Family signature_____

_____ My child may **not** attend. My child **will** attend school that day.

Family signature_____

GA1476

Resources for Teachers and Students

Fill your classroom with books that promote cooperative learning and encourage desired behavior. Check your school or public library to find books and audiovisuals which you might want to use. Add your own personal resources to those suggested below.

Bellanca, Jim. *Building a Caring, Cooperative Classroom*. Palatine, IL: Skylight Publishing, 1991.

Bennett, Barrie, Carol Rolheiser-Bennett and Laurie Stevahn. *Cooperative Learning: Where Heart Meets Mind*. Interactive Resource Books, 1991.

Gibbs, Jeanne. *Tribes, a Process for Social Development and Cooperative Learning*. Santa Rosa, CA: Center Source Publishing, 1987.

Johnson, David, Roger Johnson, Judy Bartlett, and Linda Johnson. *Our Cooperative Classroom*. Edina, MN: Interaction Book Company, 1988.

The Adventures of Lollipop Dragon (filmstrips/records) SVE, copyright 1970. (courtesy, behavior, ethics)

Below are some suggested card catalog topics for library books to read to children, available at your library. Select paperback books for children from book clubs such as Scholastic, Troll, Weekly Reader.

1. Friendship
2. Manners
3. Etiquette
4. Customs
5. Fairy tales/fables (morals)
6. Behavior
7. Listening (comprehension questions about stories read on cassette tapes or stories read aloud)
8. Following directions (origami books, arts and crafts, games)

GA1476

Quiet as a Mouse

Class Goal 5

Behavior

Line up quietly.

Face the front.

Walk properly.

Suggestions for bulletin board titles and desired behavior:
Not a Creature Was Stirring (sitting still; self-control)
"Tails" of Good Behavior (any behavior)
"EEK"citing Behavior (any behavior)
Quiet as a Mouse (working/lining up quietly)
Mice Are Nice (manners)
Actions Sp"eek" Louder Than Words (any behavior)

Suggestions for apple and mouse patterns:
Write names of individual students on apples as they exhibit
   desired behavior.
Use apple pattern for vocabulary words for any content area
   (spelling/reading words, math problems, etc.).
Enlarge mouse pattern to display behavior poems.

Mouse Pattern

GA1476

Apple Pattern

43

GA1476

Classroom Behavior Chart

Teacher_____

Behavior_____

Week of _____

Name	M	T	W	T	F
	M	T	W	T	F
	M	T	W	T	F
	M	T	W	T	F
	M	T	W	T	F
	M	T	W	T	F
	M	T	W	T	F
	M	T	W	T	F
	M	T	W	T	F
	M	T	W	T	F
	M	T	W	T	F
	M	T	W	T	F
	M	T	W	T	F
	M	T	W	T	F
	M	T	W	T	F
	M	T	W	T	F

GA1476

Conduct Card

Name _____

Date _____

Behavior _____

_____ Satisfactory

_____ Unsatisfactory

_____ Conference

_____
Parent/Guardian Signature

45

A Message from the Teacher

To:_____

From:_____Date:_____

During the past _____ our class
has been working on the following behavior:
_____. Each day
our goal was to have _____ children out of _____
show appropriate behavior in this area. When we
accomplished this, we placed an apple on our
bulletin board. Our expected goal was _____
apples. We did/did not reach this goal.

Your child received a conduct card which shows
the grade earned for_____
(behavior). When behavior was positive, no apples
were punched on his or her conduct card.
Negative behavior resulted in one apple being
punched out for each offense. Our grading system
is:

_____ – _____ "bad" apples–satisfactory

_____ – _____ "bad" apples–unsatisfactory

(____ total "good" apples possible)

Please read your child's conduct card, sign it, and
return it to school with your child tomorrow. If you
have any questions or concerns, please call me at
school at this number: _____.

Sincerely yours,

_____
(teacher)

Letter Home

Dear_____,

_____

_____

_____

_____

_____

_____

_____

_____

_____

Love,

_____

GA1476

Celebrate

Share

Enjoy a class reward. Have the children plan a few refreshments they might like to share with the class. Examples: Mice tea (use your regular iced tea recipe); Cheese and crackers (various kinds); Bite-size Three "Mouse"keteers candy bars; Mouse-shaped cookies and mice milk; Mice cream (ice-cream) bars.

Listen

Select a fiction or nonfiction book about mice to read to your class. There are numerous titles available in the school library. Your students may enjoy listening to one of these:
1. *If You Give a Mouse a Cookie* by Laura Joffe Numeroff
2. *Stewart Little* by E.B. White
3. *Mouse, Mouse Go Out of My House*, by Elizabeth Low
4. *A New House for Little Mouse* by Cindy Wheeler
5. *The Mouse and the Motorcycle* (book or video) by Beverly Cleary

Cooperate

Mice are always searching for food! Divide your class into four teams. Photocopy a complete set of apple clues for each team (there are fourteen clues total). Cut apart the apple clues and place them in a large envelope for each team to use. Send children on a scavenger hunt searching for Professor Mouse (large oaktag mouse or yourself dressed as a mouse). Children must work cooperatively to follow the clues and discover Professor Mouse. On the final clue, direct children to report to a designated spot where they will find Professor Mouse. Have children complete the scavenger hunt by finding items in the order written on the apples. Choose a small, edible treat and/or read a mouse story—perhaps one of those suggested above—to culminate the scavenger hunt!

GA1476

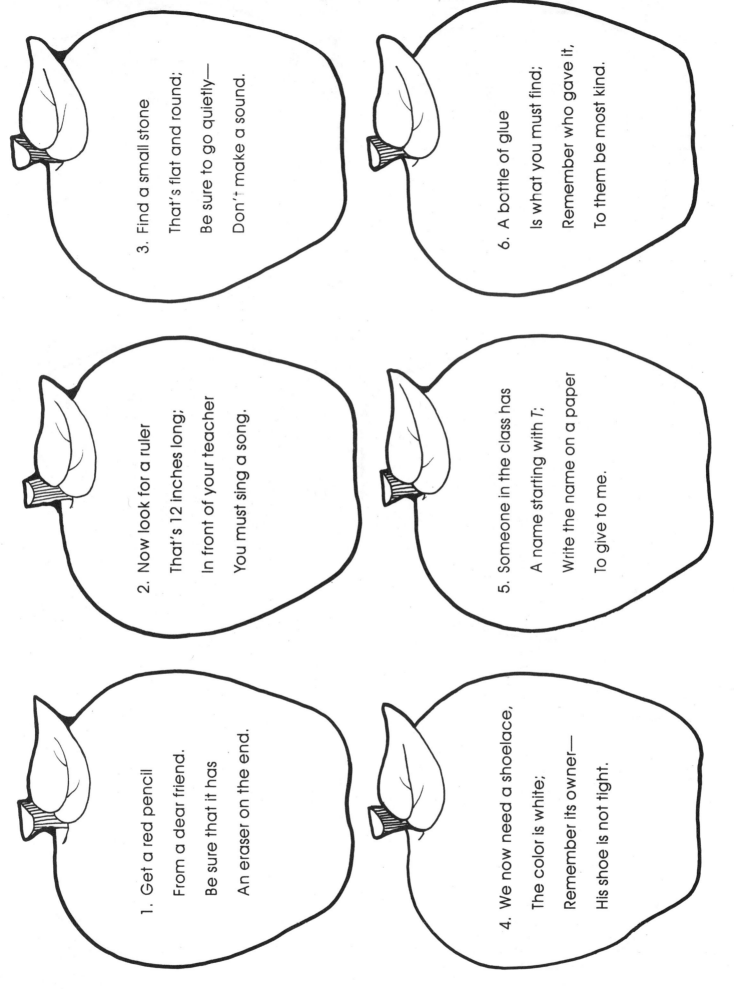

3. Find a small stone

That's flat and round;

Be sure to go quietly—

Don't make a sound.

6. A bottle of glue

Is what you must find;

Remember who gave it,

To them be most kind.

2. Now look for a ruler

That's 12 inches long;

In front of your teacher

You must sing a song.

5. Someone in the class has

A name starting with T;

Write the name on a paper

To give to me.

1. Get a red pencil

From a dear friend.

Be sure that it has

An eraser on the end.

4. We now need a shoelace,

The color is white;

Remember its owner—

His shoe is not tight.

49

GA1476

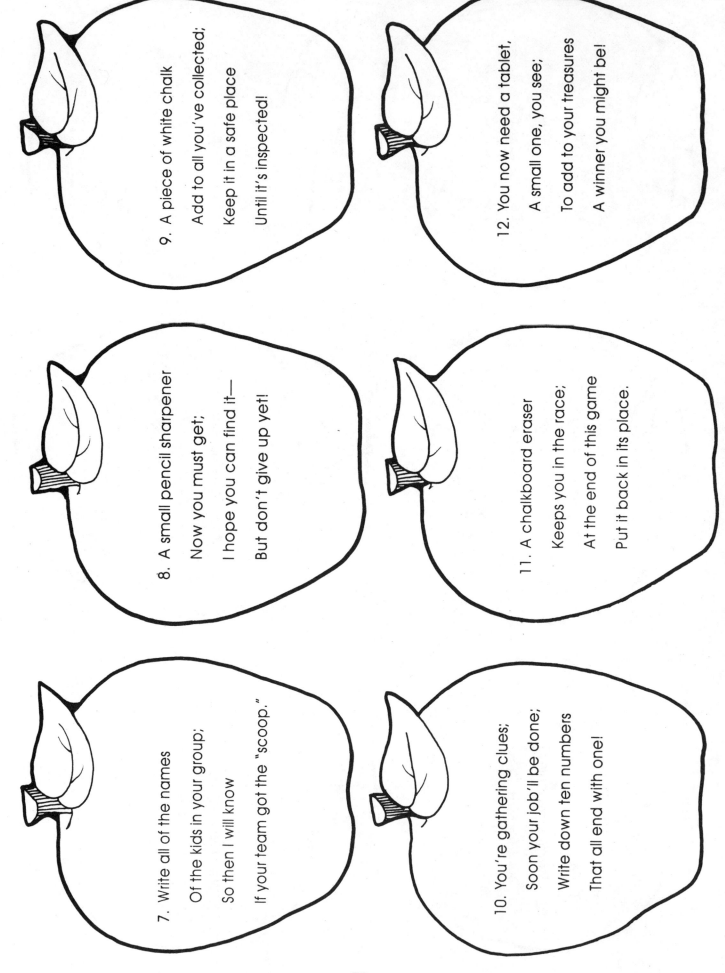

9. A piece of white chalk
   Add to all you've collected;
   Keep it in a safe place
   Until it's inspected!

12. You now need a tablet,
    A small one, you see;
    To add to your treasures
    A winner you might be!

8. A small pencil sharpener
   Now you must get;
   I hope you can find it—
   But don't give up yet!

11. A chalkboard eraser
    Keeps you in the race;
    At the end of this game
    Put it back in its place.

7. Write all of the names
   Of the kids in your group;
   So then I will know
   If your team got the "scoop."

10. You're gathering clues;
    Soon your job'll be done;
    Write down ten numbers
    That all end with one!

50

13. Pat yourself on the back,

Just one thing left to do;

Go find a paper clip;

Now on to your last clue.

14. Now find a watch (clock)

And use lots of care;

Go to the_____.

You'll find directions there.

We're "FALL"owing Good Behavior
Behavior

Raise Your Hand

Take Turns

Class Goal 5

Suggestions for bulletin board titles and desired behavior:

We Be"leaf" in Good Behavior (any behavior)
We're "FALL"owing Good Behavior (any behavior)
We're Nuts About Listening (any behavior)
We're Great at "FALL"owing Directions
"TREE"t Others with Respect
Good Behavior Is a Real "TREE"t

Suggestions for acorn and leaf patterns:

Write the child's name and the desired behavior to be exhibited on a leaf to display on the tree.

Write facts about leaves on the leaf patterns. Laminate them and display them on the tree.

Enlarge the nuts and write station ideas on each one. Display them in various locations around your room. (See page 59 for more "nutty" ideas.)

Tree Pattern

53

GA1476

Leaf Pattern

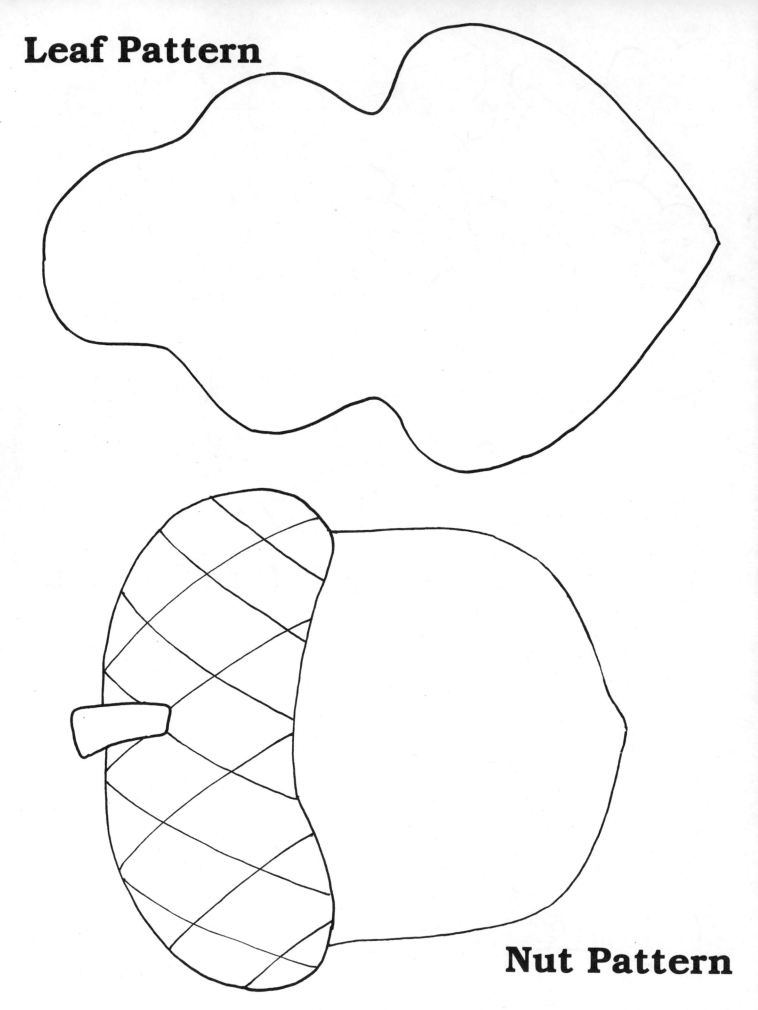

Nut Pattern

54

Classroom Behavior Chart

Teacher _____

Behavior _____

Week of _____

Name	M	T	W	T	F
	M	T	W	T	F
	M	T	W	T	F
	M	T	W	T	F
	M	T	W	T	F
	M	T	W	T	F
	M	T	W	T	F
	M	T	W	T	F
	M	T	W	T	F
	M	T	W	T	F
	M	T	W	T	F
	M	T	W	T	F
	M	T	W	T	F
	M	T	W	T	F
	M	T	W	T	F
	M	T	W	T	F

GA1476

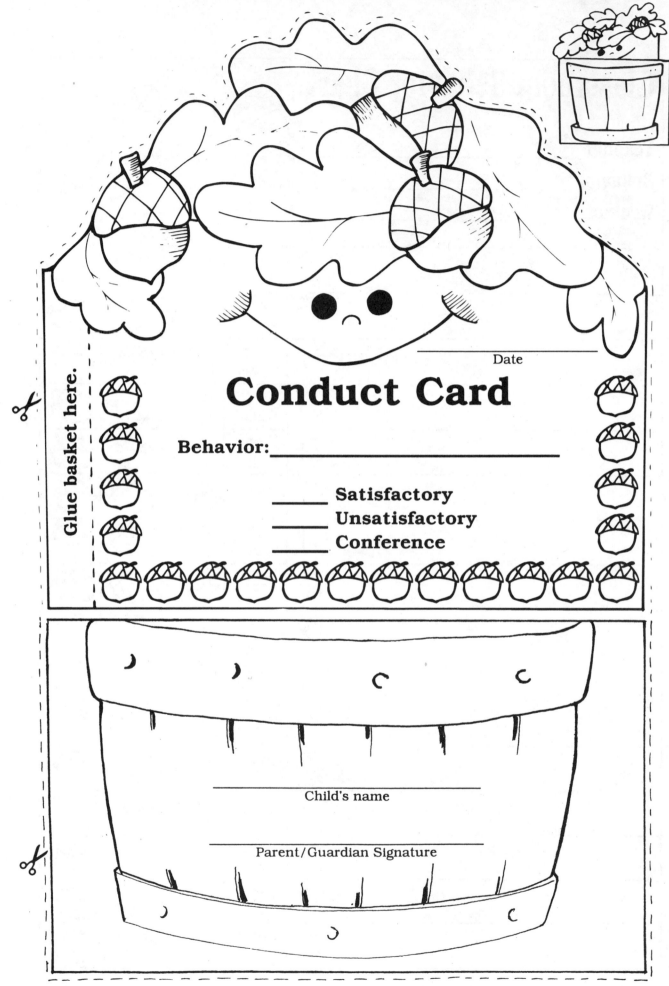

Glue basket here.

Date _____

Conduct Card

Behavior: _____

_____ **Satisfactory**
_____ **Unsatisfactory**
_____ **Conference**

_____
Child's name

_____
Parent/Guardian Signature

56

GA1476

A Message from the Teacher

To:_____

From:_____

Date:_____

During the past_____
our class has been working
on the following behavior
_____.

Each day our goal was to have _____ children out
of _____ show appropriate behavior in this area. When
we accomplished this, we placed an acorn on our bulletin
board. Our expected goal was _____ acorns. We
did/did not reach this goal.

Your child received a conduct card
which shows the grade earned
for_____ (behavior).
When behavior was positive, no acorns
were punched on his/her conduct card.
Negative behavior resulted in one acorn being
punched out for each offense. Our grading system
is:

    _____—_____ "bad" acorns–satisfactory
    _____—_____ "bad" acorns–unsatisfactory
    (___ total "good" acorns possible)

Please read your child's conduct card, sign it, and return it
to school with your child tomorrow. If your have any
questions or concerns, please call me at school at this
number: _____.

    Sincerely yours,

    _____
    (teacher)

Glue leaf.

Letter Home

by _____

58

Fun with Nuts
(Group or Independent Station Ideas)

1. Glue several different types of nuts to a piece of cardboard. Number each nut. Write the answers on the back of the cardboard. Ask children to number their papers and record the name of each nut beside the appropriate number. Have students check their responses with the answers on the back of the cardboard.

2. Create a Christmas ornament using small nuts or seeds. Fill a small, clear plastic lid with glue. Have children arrange the seeds or nuts in the gluey lid to create a seed design. Fill the entire space with one full layer. Allow the glue to dry for several days. As the glue dries, have children use a toothpick to create a small hole for the ornament hanger. When the nut mosaic is totally dry, gently peel away the plastic lid. (The glue should dry clear.) Spray the ornament lightly with shellac to make the decoration less fragile. Attach a decorative hanger and display.

3. Photocopy several acorn patterns. Write the name of a nut on each acorn in a scrambled fashion. Number each pattern. Write the correct name of the nut on the back. Laminate all of the patterns and place the acorns in a small basket in a learning center. Ask children to see how many nuts they can identify on paper. Have them check their responses.

4. Place a large container of various types of nuts in a heavy-duty plastic bag. Have the students (1) estimate the number of nuts in the bag, (2) sort the nuts and discuss with the other children each group of nuts and its attributes, (3) create some type of chart showing how the nuts were grouped, and (4) label the attributes for each group.

5. Write the name of a particular type of nut in large print on an acorn. Ask children to see how many smaller words they can find in that word.

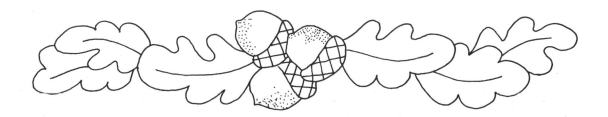

GA1476

Fun with the Fallies

Enjoy a little cooperative learning with your students. Read to them the story "The Fallies Are Coming" (pages 61-66), or provide each student with a copy of the story. Ask each group or pair to answer the questions as neatly as possible. Have each group appoint a secretary to record the group's responses. Be sure the members of each group sign their names to the paper.

Questions:

1. Who lived in Old Oak? _____

2. What two things would Wise Owl do after sunset?_____
_____

3. What was the game the leaves played?_____
_____

4. What did Wise Owl whisper to the leaves? _____
_____

5. Name four of the leaves. _____
_____

6. Why did Wise Owl tell the leaves to welcome the robins? _____
_____

7. Where did Little Tree live?_____

8. Children had fun with Little Tree. Name three things they did. _____
_____
_____
_____

9. What changes did Little Tree notice on the hillsides as he looked at the forest?_____
_____

10. What were the Fallies? _____
_____

The Fallies Are Coming

The Fallies Are Coming

Wise Owl perched high in Old Oak. He shared the tree with lively squirrels who chattered loudly as they chased one another along the weathered branches loaded with acorns. During the day he tried to sleep, but sometimes those squirrels were pretty hard to ignore. After the sunset, he would fly above the trees he guarded searching for food, keeping a watchful eye on the forest.

At the top of the hill Little Tree stretched tall, sunning his wooden head in the April air. Tiny green leaves were appearing along his skinny trunk and skyward branches. It was a game the leaves played, always waving and tilting their green heads. They loved soaking up sunshine and catching raindrops for Little Tree. They fed him when he was hungry and they always made sure he had plenty to drink. Each day Little Tree pushed his roots deeper and deeper into the rich soil. How firmly he stood when the wind ruffled his leaves and tossed him about! "Let's play! Let's play!" the leaves would beg him. Little Tree would tease them a bit and twirl them around, but he always knew when they had had enough.

One night, Little Tree was exhausted and went to bed early. Some of his leaves at the top of the tree just couldn't get to sleep. The moon was full and the stars were twinkling so brightly! The leaves were having a contest to see who could find the brightest star in the sky. Just then, Wise Owl came swooping close to them whispering, "The Fallies are coming! The Fallies are coming!"

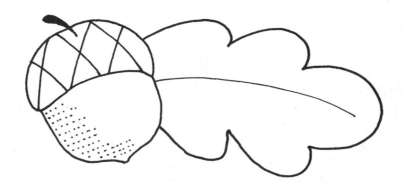

GA1476

"What are Fallies?"
wondered Oakey from his
place at the top of the tree. "I don't
know," answered another leaf. "Will they hurt
us?" questioned another. "I'm scared," said Rusty. "Me
too," said another leaf. When Oakey looked up to ask Wise
Owl, he had already flown past Little Tree. The leaves talked
about the Fallies late into the night, and then all was quiet.

The next morning the leaves began quizzing Little Tree about
Wise Owl's message. Not even Little Tree was sure what the Fallies
were, and, not wanting to scare his leaves, he promised them that it
must be something wonderful!

As the days passed, the leaves grew broader and sturdier.
They began to enjoy the breezes and refreshing showers. When the
sun lit the sky, Little Tree covered the ground with his tiny blanket
of shade. The leaves would open wide to cool the warm earth. They
were proud to be getting so big! The leaves would watch one
another's shadows dance on the ground below. "Someday," thought
Ashley, "my shadow will be the biggest of all." "And mine," said
Hazel, "will be just like yours."

There was a noise on the branch over their heads, and the
leaves looked up. "It's nice and cool here," said Wise Owl. "Mind if I
join you for awhile?"

Ashley, Hazel, and the others chatted about the birds busily
building nests on Little Tree's branches. "Welcome them," said Wise
Owl. "Those robins will keep you company for a long time!" Just
before Wise Owl flew away he reminded the leaves, "The Fallies are
coming! The Fallies are coming!"

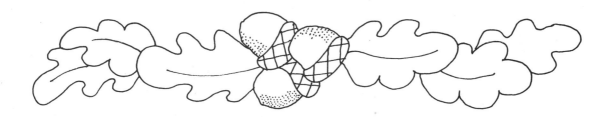

Too quickly Wise
Owl had gone, and the leaves
were once again curious. "What does
Wise Owl mean? Why does he always say
that?" asked Filbert. Little Tree chimed in, "He has a
surprise waiting for all of us, but he wants to keep it a
secret. He tells me that the Fallies are really grand! To be
invited you each must do something very special! You must be
something very special!"

The leaves listened to Little Tree speak, but they were so
excited about their new guest that they soon forgot about the
Fallies. The robins, indeed, were good company. When the forest
was silent, the robins sang sweetly and flitted about. They seemed
to like their new home. When the weather grew stormy, the leaves
huddled together to protect the young birds. And when the sun
shone too brightly, the leaves shaded the little nest. How happy
they were to share their home!

By midsummer, Little Tree had grown so much. He stretched
a little taller and reached out a little wider. He had so many leaves
now that he sometimes lost count. From the top of the hill he had a
wonderful view of the valley below. He felt a little braver, a little
stronger, and a little wiser than he had in early spring.

Little Tree awoke from his nap one day just in time to see
children climbing the hill toward him. They began winding their
way up the wooded path. Soon they were chasing one another
around and around his trunk. Then they began tugging on the
lowest branches. "This is fun! Give me a push and I can reach a
little higher!" giggled Olive. The children were delighted! Little Tree
was the perfect tree. Higher and higher the children climbed,
swinging on the branches and daring one another up. Laurel found
a seat beside Willow, and they sat for a long time sharing secrets
while the others played on the ground below. The leaves listened to

64

GA1476

their tales with
glee, and they longed to enjoy
some of the adventures the two girls
had shared. "How nice it would be to travel
and explore!" thought the leaves. "Just think of all of
the exciting places we could go!" They dreamed one dream
after another. Soon Laurel and Willow joined the others on the
ground for a game of tag before they disappeared into the forest.
When evening came, Wise Owl stopped to rest in a nearby tree.
Some of the leaves heard him hoot, "The Fallies are coming! The
Fallies are coming!"

Little Tree was awakened early the next morning by all of the
commotion the leaves were making. They were discussing how crisp
and damp they felt! Little Tree noticed that the leaves that were
once Christmas green were changing. "Wise Owl! Wise Owl!" he
called. "Something magical is happening! My leaves are changing
color!"

"The Fallies are coming!" Wise Owl hooted as he flew to a
branch next to Little Tree's trunk. "It won't be long now! Don't
worry, Little Tree. I'll keep watch over you." He snuggled a little
closer to the trunk, paused a moment, and then flew away.

Little Tree searched his branches daily to notice the last green
leaf change color. It seemed that the autumn sun was playing tricks
on him. As he looked around the forest, he saw that beautifully
colored trees dotted the hillsides. Golden grasses covered the earth.
How proud Little Tree was of his new coat! He couldn't help but feel
happy about the change that had taken place. The leaves danced
recklessly in the brisk air as if to show off their new colors. Little
Tree couldn't remember when he felt happier!

GA1476

One chilly night
the wind blew hard and Little
Tree noticed the cool air stirring his
branches. His leaves shook in the dark, and he
wished the moon could warm him in the night as the
sun did during the day. A bit scared, Little Tree soon fell
asleep. When he awoke, he felt a warmth around his roots.
Looking down, he was saddened to find that many of his leaves had
blown from his branches. Rusty, Olive, Myrtle, Willow, and several
others lay piled around his trunk. There were bare spots on his
limbs. "Wise Owl! Wise Owl!" he cried. "Something's wrong!"

The leaves at Little Tree's feet seemed so excited! They were
tossed about by the wind and seemed to be laughing and playing.
Little Tree felt so confused. He knew that his leaves loved him! So
why did they leave? Wise Owl talked softly to him. "The Fallies are
here! The Fallies are here!" he explained. "Every year when your
new coat shines brightest of all, your leaves will make you proud.
They will signal to the forest that you have been a good tree! You
lifted them high toward the sun where they could grow and enjoy
life. They, in return, fed you and protected you. They brought new
life to your branches. They warmed you and cooled you as the
seasons changed. Don't be sad! Those leaves must leave you, Little
Tree. But there will be another day when the warm sun will fill your
branches with new green leaves, new friends. There will be many
leaves and many Fallies, year after year after year. Those leaves you
see on the ground now are preparing for a new life on their own.
Their greatest adventures are about to begin!

CELEBRATE

Get your class into the fall spirit as you enjoy these activities. Games can be played in large or small groups, indoors or out.

1. Acorn Toss—Have each child choose a partner. Partners stand facing each other just a short distance apart. One player tosses the acorn to the partner. If the partner catches it, he or she moves one step backward. He or she then tosses the acorn back. If that partner catches it, he or she steps backward one step. When either partner drops the acorn, the two-person team is disqualified. The winning team is the team that moves the farthest distance apart without dropping the acorn.

2. Acorn Drop—Place a large, wide-mouth bottle (plastic) on the floor. Find about ten to twenty acorns. Ask children to stand in single file behind the bottle and see which child can drop the most acorns in the bottle. (Use more bottles if you have a large class.)

3. Raking the Leaves—Divide your class into two or more teams. Seat each team in single file at one end of the room. At the opposite end, place a bushel basket and a rake for each team. Pile several leaves on the floor around each basket. At the whistle, the first player on each team runs to the basket, begins raking leaves, and puts them into the basket. Player one runs back. Player two runs down, empties the basket, runs back and the process repeats. (Odd players fill the basket; even players empty it.) The winning team has all players complete the activity first.

A Harvest of Good Listeners

Behavior

| Listen to Teacher | Listen to Others |

Class Goal
5

Suggestions for bulletin board titles and desired behavior:
    Good Behavior Is Plentiful (any behavior)
    A Harvest of Good Listeners
    Grade "A" Turkeys (any behavior)
    A Crop of Good Students (any behavior)
    Harvesting Good Citizens
    We Have Plenty to Brag About (any behavior)

Suggestions for turkey, hat, and fruit patterns:
    Enlarge the turkey and write appropriate behavior poems on separate turkey patterns to display.
    Make several hat patterns and write special "Hats Off for Good Behavior" messages to children who deserve recognition or encouragement.
    Photocopy on oaktag at least twenty of each type of fruit.
    Use it to create the learning center found on page 76.

Turkey Pattern

69

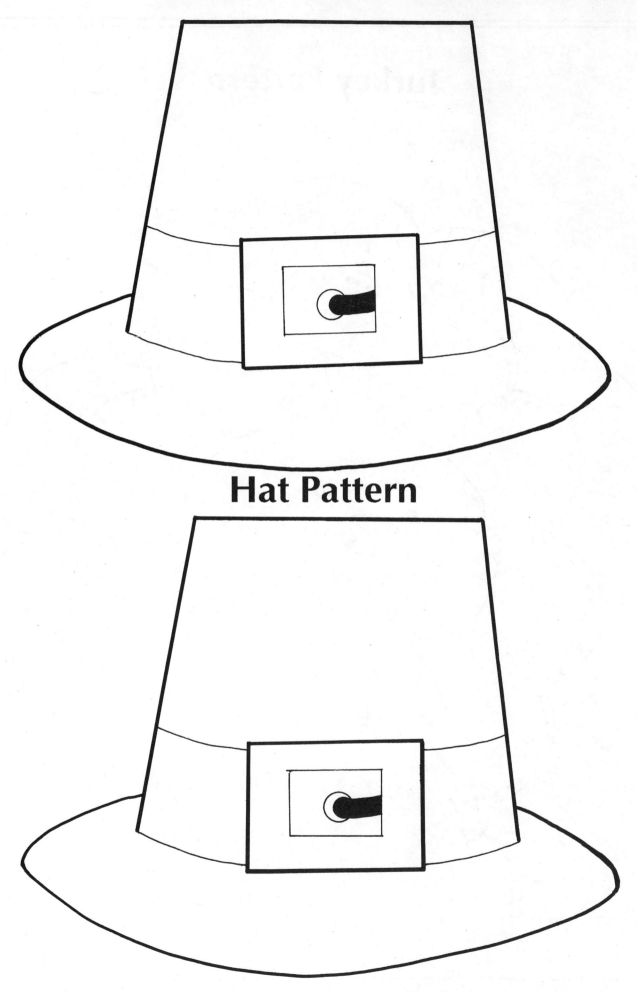

Hat Pattern

Fruit Patterns

GA1476

Classroom Behavior Chart

Teacher _____

Behavior _____

Week of _____

Name	M	T	W	T	F
	M	T	W	T	F
	M	T	W	T	F
	M	T	W	T	F
	M	T	W	T	F
	M	T	W	T	F
	M	T	W	T	F
	M	T	W	T	F
	M	T	W	T	F
	M	T	W	T	F
	M	T	W	T	F
	M	T	W	T	F
	M	T	W	T	F
	M	T	W	T	F
	M	T	W	T	F
	M	T	W	T	F

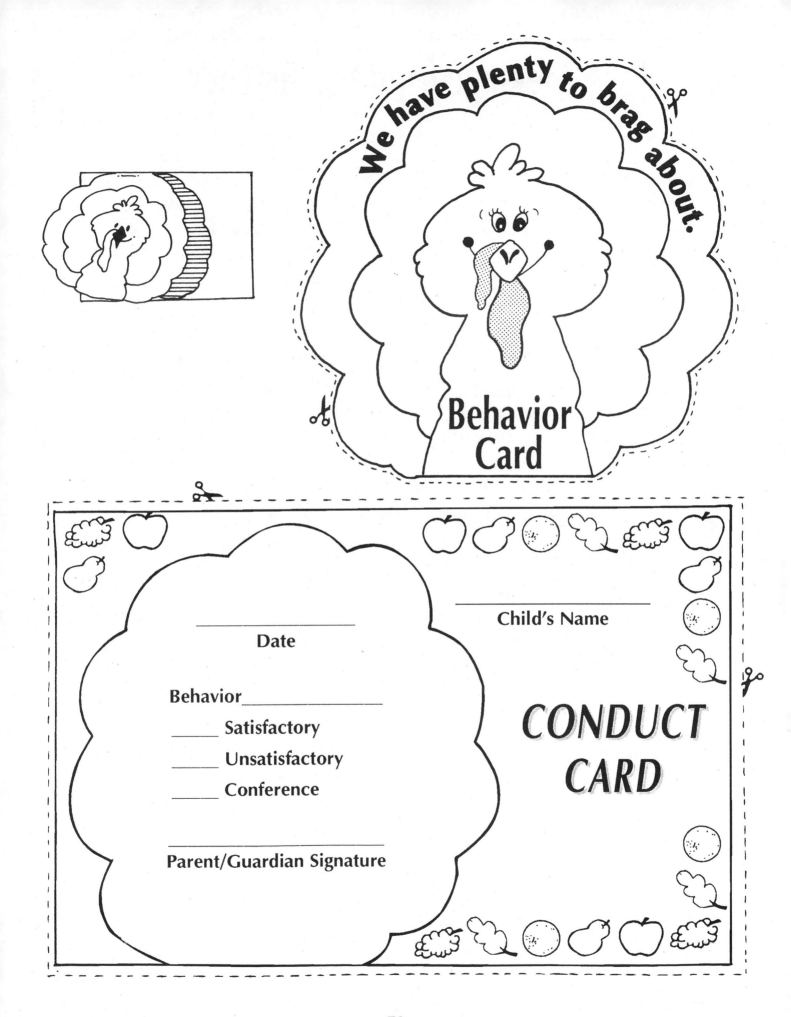

We have plenty to brag about.

Behavior Card

Child's Name

Date

Behavior_____

_____ Satisfactory

_____ Unsatisfactory

_____ Conference

_____
Parent/Guardian Signature

CONDUCT CARD

73

A Message from the Teacher

To:_____

From:_____ Date:_____

During the past_____our class has been working on the following behavior:_____. Each day our goal was to have_____children out of_____show appropriate behavior in this area. When we accomplished this, we placed a piece of fruit on our bulletin board. Our expected goal was _____pieces of fruit. We did/did not reach this goal.

Your child received a conduct card which shows the grade earned for_____(behavior). When behavior was positive, no pieces of fruit were punched on his/her conduct card. Negative behavior resulted in one piece of fruit being punched out for each offense. Our grading system is:

____-____"bad" fruit—SATISFACTORY

____-____"bad" fruit—UNSATISFACTORY

(_____total "good" fruit possible)

Please read your child's conduct card, sign it, and return it to school with your child immediately. If you have any questions or concerns, please call me at this number:

_____

_____School

Sincerely yours,

_____

Letter Home

_____
Date

Dear_____,

_____

_____

_____

_____

_____

_____

           _____

           _____

           _____

           _____

           Love,

           _____

Plenty of Fun . . .

Use the fruit patterns found on page 71 to create this fun learning center for language arts. You will need to photocopy on oaktag eighteen patterns of each piece of fruit. Cut out the fruit. On the apple pattern write the sentence starters from column 1 below; on the grape pattern write the predicates from column 2; on the pear pattern copy the sentence endings from column 3. Laminate all the fruit and place it in a small basket at a learning center in your room. Have children choose three different pieces of fruit and arrange them to form a sentence. Ask children to write down the sentences they collect. For more experienced students, you might want to make the assignment more difficult by asking children to complete one or more additional activities: (1) label all nouns found in their sentences; (2) identify the complete/simple subjects and predicates; (3) label all parts of speech; (4) identify verb tense, etc.

1	2	3
my brother	practiced basketball	in the gym
Jeremy's dog	chased a Frisbee™	in the park
Grandma	baked a cake	for my birthday
Ronnie	traded baseball cards	with my friend
his mom	bought a piano	at the mall
the robin	sang a sweet song	in the tree
Grandpa	caught a trout	in the stream
my family	built a cabin	in the woods
the tiny pup	buried a bone	under the porch
Mom	bought a present	for Dad
my babysitter	played a game	with my brothers
Nancy	built a snowman	in the yard
Dad	parked my truck	in that garage
the park ranger	took my family	on a nature hike
Debbie	lost her ring	in the pool
Uncle Brad	collected seashells	at the beach
my cousin Josh	ate lunch	at McDonald's
the farmer	dug a deep hole	in the garden

Get your class into a festive mood by playing the game "Fruit Basket." Choose the names of five or six types of fruit. Whisper the name of one of the fruits in each child's ear. After all children have been assigned a fruit, call out the name of one of the fruits that you chose. Each child with that name must exchange seats with another player before a designated time has elapsed. Players who fail to find a new seat are put into the "fruit bowl" (area of the room where they stay during the game). When you say "fruit basket upset," all children must exchange places before time is up.

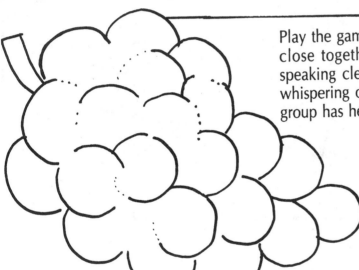

Play the game Grapevine (like gossip). Seat your class in a circle, close together. Whisper a message into the first player's ear, speaking clearly and slowly. That player repeats the message by whispering one time to the next player and so on until the entire group has heard it. The last player tells the class what message he or she heard. (Discuss with your class that rumors begin this way and that often the gossip they hear has been changed in this manner.)

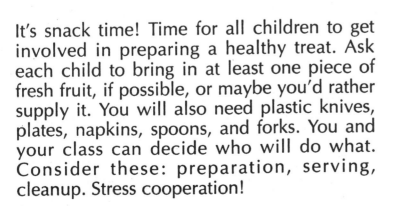

It's snack time! Time for all children to get involved in preparing a healthy treat. Ask each child to bring in at least one piece of fresh fruit, if possible, or maybe you'd rather supply it. You will also need plastic knives, plates, napkins, spoons, and forks. You and your class can decide who will do what. Consider these: preparation, serving, cleanup. Stress cooperation!

GA1476

Wishing for Good Manners

Target Behavior
1. In the cafeteria
2. In the bathroom
3. On the bus

Class Goal
10

Suggestions for bulletin board titles and desired behavior:
Star Delight (any behavior)
Delightful Stars (any behavior)
We're Shining Brightly (any behavior)
"STAR"ring the Best Citizens
Wishing for Good Manners

Suggestions for snowman and star patterns:
Enlarge the snowman and make several large patterns. Display behavior poems on them to hang around the room as wall decorations. Place several snowmen together and title the scene "Snowmen on Parade."

Photocopy several star patterns. Use them for math stations. Number the stars, beginning with zero and ending with fifty. Create stations for addition, multiplication, patterning, even/odd, etc.

Enlarge a star pattern to use for your dedication of star of the week (teacher's helper, top student, most improved, other).

GA1476

Snowman Pattern

GA1476

Star Patterns

80

GA1476

Classroom Behavior Chart

Teacher _____

Behavior _____

Week of _____

Name	M	T	W	T	F
	M	T	W	T	F
	M	T	W	T	F
	M	T	W	T	F
	M	T	W	T	F
	M	T	W	T	F
	M	T	W	T	F
	M	T	W	T	F
	M	T	W	T	F
	M	T	W	T	F
	M	T	W	T	F
	M	T	W	T	F
	M	T	W	T	F
	M	T	W	T	F
	M	T	W	T	F
	M	T	W	T	F
	M	T	W	T	F

Conduct Card

Name _____

Date _____

Behavior _____

_____ Satisfactory

_____ Unsatisfactory

_____ Conference

_____
Parent/Guardian Signature

GA1476

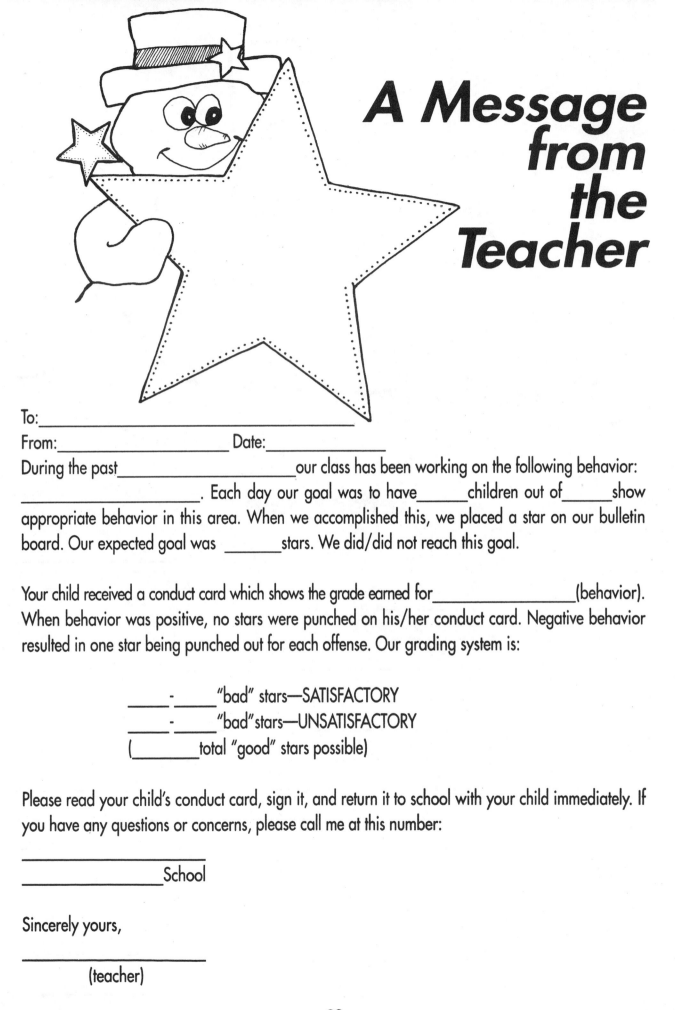

A Message from the Teacher

To:_____

From:_____ Date:_____

During the past_____our class has been working on the following behavior:

_____ . Each day our goal was to have_____children out of_____show

appropriate behavior in this area. When we accomplished this, we placed a star on our bulletin

board. Our expected goal was _____stars. We did/did not reach this goal.

Your child received a conduct card which shows the grade earned for_____(behavior).

When behavior was positive, no stars were punched on his/her conduct card. Negative behavior

resulted in one star being punched out for each offense. Our grading system is:

_____-_____"bad" stars—SATISFACTORY

_____-_____"bad"stars—UNSATISFACTORY

(_____total "good" stars possible)

Please read your child's conduct card, sign it, and return it to school with your child immediately. If

you have any questions or concerns, please call me at this number:

_____

_____School

Sincerely yours,

_____

(teacher)

Letter Home

_____
Date

Dear_____,

_____

_____

_____

_____

_____

_____

_____

Love,

_____

84

GA1476

Roll a Snowman

To make this tube snowman you will need:
    crayons or markers
    glue
    scissors

Directions:
1. Cut out the large rectangle on the next page along the solid outer lines.
2. Color the snowman's face and star buttons.
3. Glue the area shown. Roll the paper into a tube and press firmly on the glued area. This forms the snowman's body.
4. Color and cut out the hat and scarf and glue them to the snowman's body.
5. Attach a broom, mittens, or other items if you choose.

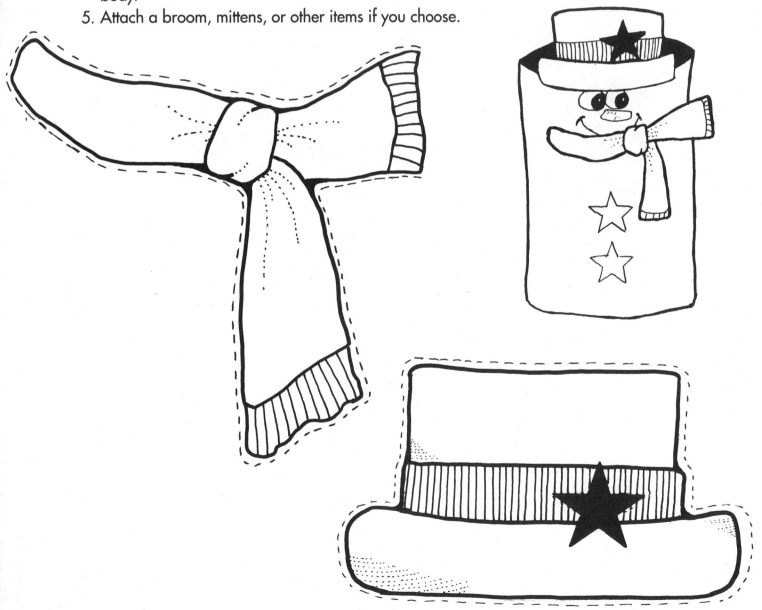

          GA1476

Cooperative Learning Fun

There are numerous ways to set up cooperative learning groups in your classroom. Here is one you may want to try as children create the snowmen on pages 85-86. (Don't hesitate to use your own ideas for establishing group work. Choose strategies that fit your teaching situation and age level. You know your students best!)

Divide your class into groups of four children. In each group select:

1. Supplier—a person who gets all of the supplies the group needs and returns them to their proper places.

2. Cleanup—a person who makes sure that the work area is clean and all materials have been given to the supplier to be put away.

3. Manager—a person who oversees that all students in the group carry out their jobs.

4. Encourager—a person who keeps all group members on task and offers help, praise, or encouragement to others in the group.

- It is a good idea to form heterogeneous groups.

- It is a good idea to rotate jobs so that all children have a chance to sharpen social talents in many areas.

It is essential that the teacher oversees all groups, takes both positive and negative notes about behavior observed, and shares recorded observations with the class!

GA1476

Create snowmen for your classroom using the ideas presented on the following pages. Display the completed artwork. They make darling centerpieces for tables in the lunchroom or classroom!

Plan a "Build-a-Snowman Contest." Encourage all children to become involved in building the snow creature. Encourage children to give their snowmen names and to be creative builders!

Assemble a "class book" by asking each student to write a one-page autobiography. Illustrations are welcome. Compile the pages, add a cover, and title the book "Starring Mr./Mrs. _____'s Class." Let children take turns sharing the book with their families at home.

CELEBRATE

Photocopy enough star patterns so that every two children in the class have ten. Working in pairs, ask the class to research a particular constellation. Have children write one fact on each star. (They could also write general star facts if they choose.) Assign each group a designated area to display their constellations. Allow time to "enjoy the sky!"

88

GA1476

Good Behavior Is Catchy

Behavior
Complete Classwork
Complete Homework

Class Goal 5

Suggestions for bulletin board titles and desired behavior:
>   Good Behavior Is Catchy (any behavior)
>   Caught with Good Behavior (any behavior)
>   A Great Catch (any behavior)
>   Hooked on Listening (any behavior)
>   Fishing for Good Citizens
>   A N"ice" Catch (any behavior)

Suggestions for penguin and fish patterns:
>   Enlarge the penguins and display desired behavior poems on them to hang in strategic places around your classroom.

>   Photocopy several fish patterns. See if your students can follow oral directions. On each fish write three or more directions that children could perform. (See suggestions on pages 95 and 96.) Place all fish in a small fishbowl. Ask a student to select a fish from the bowl, hand it to you to read orally to the class, and perform it without error. Compile sets of your own directions to challenge your students!

GA1476

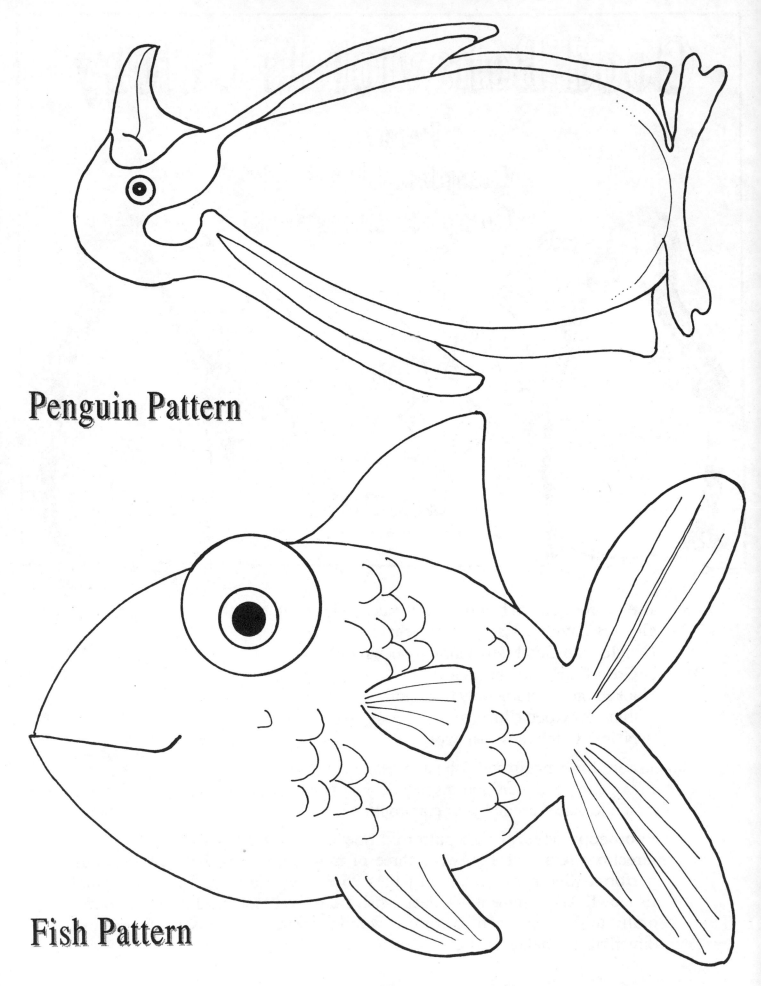

Penguin Pattern

Fish Pattern

90

Classroom Behavior Chart

Teacher _____

Behavior _____

Week of _____

Name	M	T	W	T	F
	M	T	W	T	F
	M	T	W	T	F
	M	T	W	T	F
	M	T	W	T	F
	M	T	W	T	F
	M	T	W	T	F
	M	T	W	T	F
	M	T	W	T	F
	M	T	W	T	F
	M	T	W	T	F
	M	T	W	T	F
	M	T	W	T	F
	M	T	W	T	F
	M	T	W	T	F
	M	T	W	T	F

GA1476

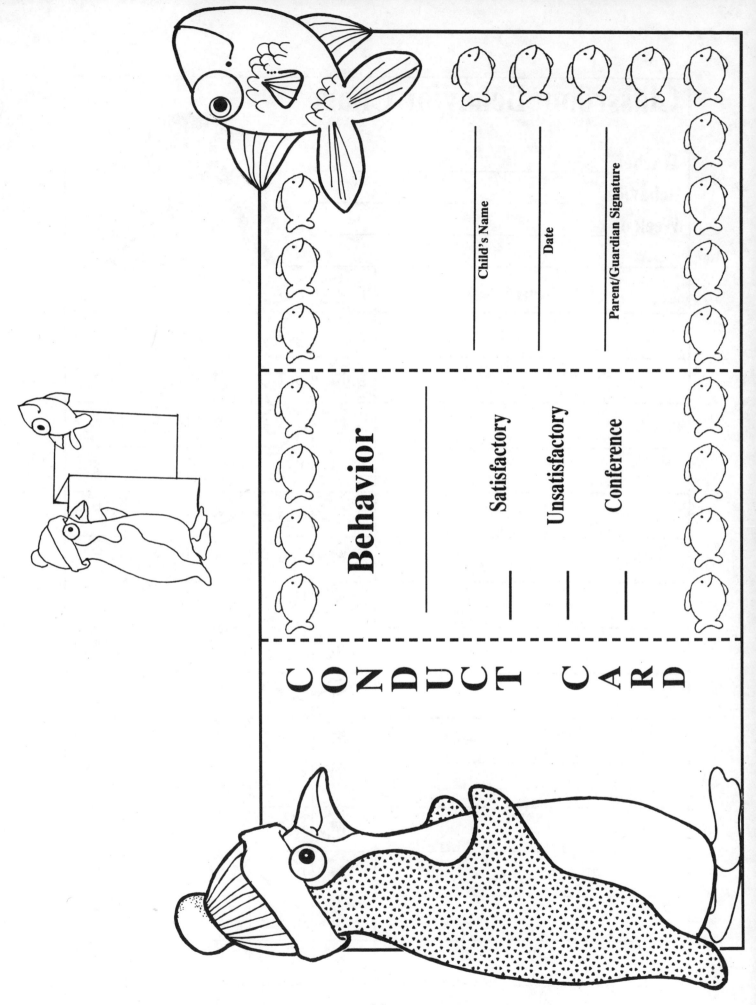

CONDUCT CARD

Behavior

___ Satisfactory

___ Unsatisfactory

___ Conference

_____
Child's Name

_____
Date

_____
Parent/Guardian Signature

A Message from the Teacher

To:_____

From:_____ Date:_____

During the past _____ our class has been working on the following behavior_____.
Each day our goal was to have _____ children out of _____ show appropriate behavior in this area. When we accomplished this, we placed a fish on our bulletin board. Our expected goal was_____ fish. We did/did not reach this goal.

Your child received a conduct card which shows the grade earned for _____ (behavior).
When behavior was positive, no fish were punched on his/her conduct card. Negative behavior resulted in one fish being punched for each offense. Our grading system is:

    ____-____ "bad" fish–satisfactory

    ____-____ "bad" fish–unsatisfactory

    (_____ total "good" fish possible)

Please read your child's conduct card, sign it, and return it to school with your child tomorrow. If you have any questions or concerns, please call me at school at this number: _____.

Sincerely yours,

_____
(teacher)

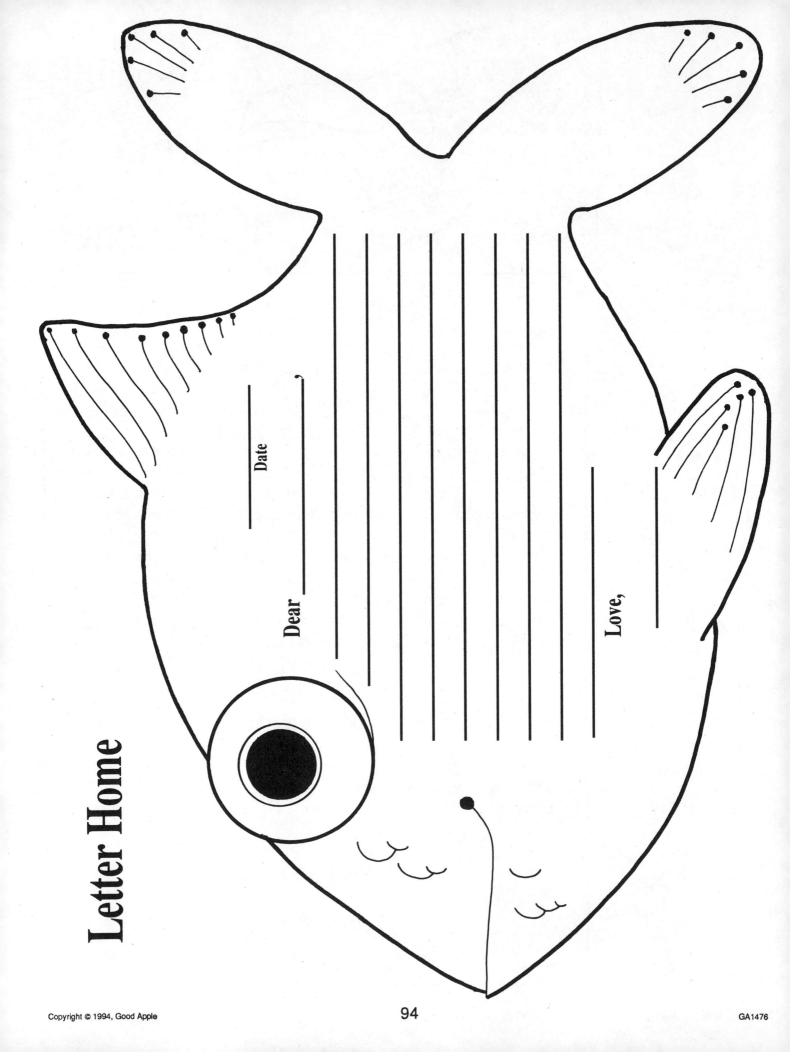

Letter Home

Date _____

Dear _____

Love,

94

GA1476

Oral Directions

Following **oral directions** is a skill you'll want to practice with your students throughout the entire year. Begin with short clues so that children will experience success and develop an attitude for good listening. Lengthen the clues as your class improves. Create your own clues to add to those listed below to make them appropriate for your grade level. Challenge your students to add their own for the class to try!

1. Stand by your chair. Tell the class your first and last name. Sit down and put your head down.

2. Walk to the front of the classroom. Write your last name on the board. Sit down and put your hands in your lap.

3. Skip to your teacher. Shake his or her right hand with your right hand. Hop to your seat and sit down.

4. Walk to your friend's chair. Whisper something in his or her ear. Take giant steps back to your seat and sit down.

5. Hop to the chalkboard. Write your favorite hobby on the board. Tell the class why you like it best. Walk to your seat and sit down.

6. Stand by your chair. Turn around three times. Recite your ABCs. Now sit down.

7. Stand behind your chair. Give the class a report about today's weather. Name your favorite season. Sit down.

8. Walk over to a friend and shake his or her hand. Ask how he or she is today. After the answer, skip back to your chair.

9. Tiptoe to the chalkboard. Write the month of your birthday on the board. Tell the class the best present you ever got for your birthday and why. Tiptoe back to your chair.

10. Stand by your chair. Tell the class three things you would like them to know about you. Turn around once and sit down.

11. Go to the front of the classroom. Tell the class the name of your favorite book. Name three things that happen in the story. Hop back to your seat.

12. Stand. Touch your toes five times. Do three jumping jacks. Hop four times. Sit down.

13. Walk to your teacher and say the name of your favorite subject. Tell what you like best about the subject and why. Skip back to your seat.

14. Name a friend. Ask your friend to go to the chalkboard with you. Both of you write the numbers from one to twenty. Circle the number that tells your age. Sit down.

15. Stand by your desk. Count by twos up to fifty. Turn around twice. Sit down.

16. Skip to the chalkboard. Write down the name of the place you would like to go on vacation. Tell the class why you would enjoy this place. Tap your friend on the head. Sit down.

17. Walk to the chalkboard. Draw a picture to represent your favorite holiday. Ask a classmate to guess the name of the holiday. Tiptoe to your seat.

18. Write your favorite color on the chalkboard. Name three things that are that color. Circle the third one. Walk back to your seat.

19. Hop over to your teacher and wish him or her a good day. Tell your teacher today's date. Write today's date correctly on the chalkboard. Do five jumping jacks. Sit down.

GA1476

Motivate your students to follow directions by creating the fishbowl activity and playing it with the class. Try it several times using the ideas given on pages 95-96. Be sure to supplement those suggested by your students with additional ideas of your own.

Select a story about fish or penguins to read aloud to your class. Stop along the way and ask children to predict what they think might happen next in the story. Place a variety of fish or penguin books in your classroom for students to enjoy.

Celebrate

Play the game Simon Says with your class. You be Simon and keep the game moving quickly to hold interest. Even older children will enjoy the challenge. After a few times, ask a student to be Simon. (A great game for following directions!)

Visit a local pet store or invite a pet store owner to your classroom to discuss fish as pets and how to properly care for them.

GA1476

"Bear"y Good Students

**Behavior
In the Cafeteria
In the Hallway**

**Class Goal
5**

Suggestions for bulletin board titles and desired behavior:
   Bear Hugs for Good Behavior (any behavior)
   Bear in Mind That We've Been Good (any behavior)
   "Bear"y Good Students (any behavior)
   We're "Bear"y Good Listeners
   We Bear Tidings of Goodness (any behavior)
   A "Bear"y Exciting Class (any behavior)

Suggestions for using bear patterns:
   Enlarge bears and display desired behavior poems on them.
   Photocopy several bears to use as flash cards for any content area.
      Laminate them to make them more durable.
   Photocopy several bears. On the back of each bear, write a word
      associated with bears for a writing bank that children could use
      at a creative writing center. Examples: hibernate, cubs, honey,
      mammal, etc.

98   GA1476

Bear Patterns

GA1476

Classroom Behavior Chart

Teacher _____

Behavior _____

Week of _____

Name	M	T	W	T	F
	M	T	W	T	F
	M	T	W	T	F
	M	T	W	T	F
	M	T	W	T	F
	M	T	W	T	F
	M	T	W	T	F
	M	T	W	T	F
	M	T	W	T	F
	M	T	W	T	F
	M	T	W	T	F
	M	T	W	T	F
	M	T	W	T	F
	M	T	W	T	F
	M	T	W	T	F
	M	T	W	T	F

GA1476

Conduct Card

Name_____

Date_____

Behavior _____

_____ **Satisfactory**
_____ **Unsatisfactory**
_____ **Conference**

_____
Parent/Guardian Signature

A Message from the Teacher

To: _____

From: _____ Date: _____

During the past _____ our class has been working on the following behavior: _____.
Each day our goal was to have _____ children out of _____ show appropriate behavior in this area. When we accomplished this, we placed a heart on our bulletin board. Our expected goal was _____ hearts. We did/did not reach this goal.

Your child received a conduct card which shows the grade earned for_____ (behavior). When behavior was positive, no hearts were punched on his/her conduct card. Negative behavior resulted in one heart being punched for each offense. Our grading system is:

_____-_____ "bad" hearts–satisfactory

_____-_____ "bad" hearts–unsatisfactory

(_____ total "good" hearts possible)

Please read your child's conduct card, sign it, and return it to school with your child tomorrow. If your have any questions or concerns, please call me at school at this number:_____.

Sincerely yours,

_____

(teacher)

GA1476

Letter Home

Date _____

Dear _____,

Love,

_____

103

Celebrate

Make bear-shaped sugar cookies with your class. Use a parent helper if necessary. (Or make the bear cookies at home and take them to school for the children to decorate.) Use tubes of icing to add decorations. Children may enjoy personalizing their bears by writing their names on them.

Read several books about bears to your students. There are numerous fiction and nonfiction books available. Here are three books by Stan and Jan Berenstain that you may enjoy reading to the class: (1) *The Berenstain Bears Forget Their Manners* (New York: Random House for Young Readers, 1985), (2) *The Berenstain Bears and the Truth* (New York: Random House for Young Readers, 1988), (3) *The Berenstain Bears and Mama's New Job* (New York: Random House for Young Readers, 1984). All three books could be used not only for entertainment, but to promote class discussions as well.

Display several nonfiction books about bears in your room. Photocopy several bears using the patterns on page 99. On the front of each bear, write a question about bears. Let students work with partners to research answers to the questions. Have children write the answers to the questions on the backs of their bears. Allow time for children to present their findings to the class. Provide a small "honey pot" near your book display in which bear question and answer cards can be kept for individual use.

Blooming Citizens

**Class Goal
10**

Behavior
Respect Your Own Property
Respect the Property
of Others

Suggestions for bulletin board titles and desired behavior:
A Great Bunch (any behavior)
We Picked the Best (any behavior)
Blooming Citizens (or any behavior)
How Is Your Garden Growing? (any behavior)
A Bouquet for_____(teacher's name) (any behavior)
A Bouquet of Good Behavior

Suggestions for using tulip and rabbit patterns:
Enlarge the rabbit pattern and use it to display poems for desired behavior.
Fold a large piece of light-colored construction paper in half. Glue the rabbit pattern to the front of the paper to create a greeting card for someone special. (The tulip pattern could also be used on the card).
Photocopy several tulips using the pattern on page 107. Write the name of each child and a brief note about his or her appropriate behavior. Display the tulips in a "garden" on your classroom bulletin board, on the wall of the classroom, or along the baseboard in the hallway for all to see!

Rabbit Pattern

Tulip/Leaf Pattern

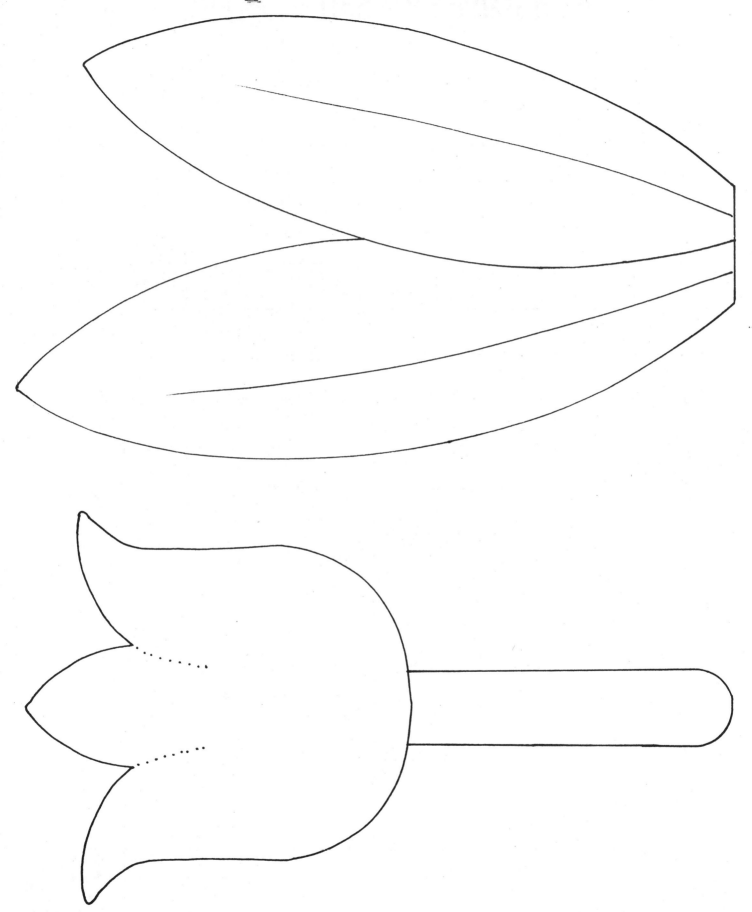

107

GA1476

Classroom Behavior Chart

Teacher _____

Behavior _____

Week of _____

Name	M	T	W	T	F
	M	T	W	T	F
	M	T	W	T	F
	M	T	W	T	F
	M	T	W	T	F
	M	T	W	T	F
	M	T	W	T	F
	M	T	W	T	F
	M	T	W	T	F
	M	T	W	T	F
	M	T	W	T	F
	M	T	W	T	F
	M	T	W	T	F
	M	T	W	T	F
	M	T	W	T	F

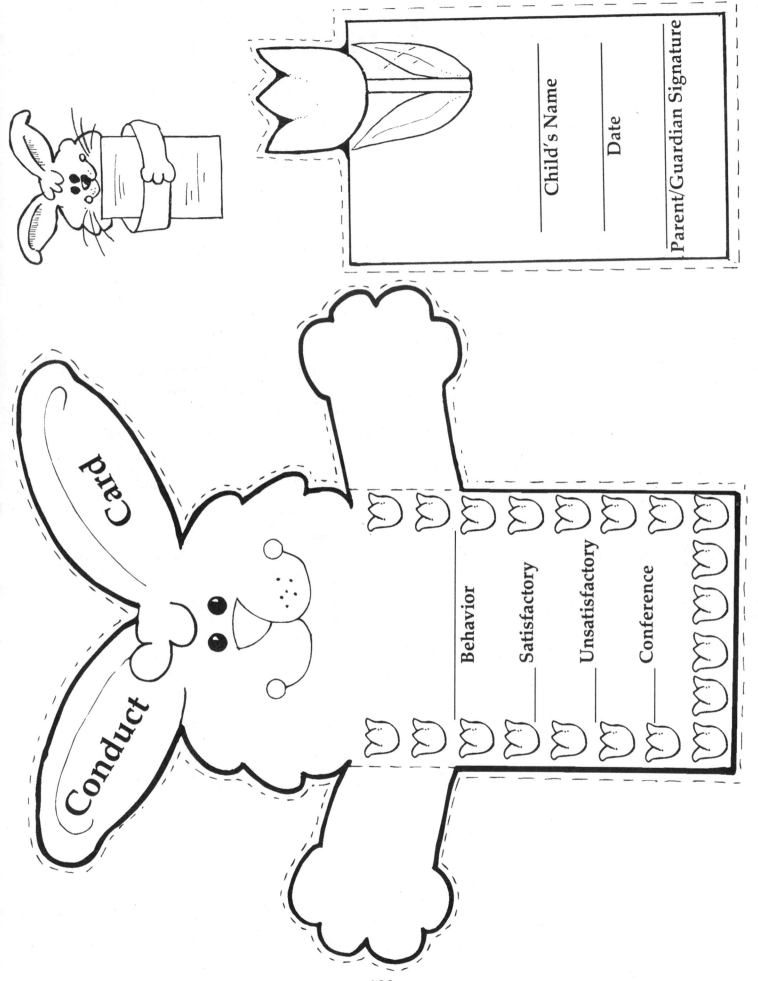

Conduct Card

Child's Name

Date

Parent/Guardian Signature

Behavior

Satisfactory

Unsatisfactory

Conference

GA1476

A Message from the Teacher

To:_____

From:_____Date:_____

During the past _____ our class has been working on
the following behavior: _____. Each
day our goal was to have _____ children out of _____ show appropriate
behavior in this area. When we accomplished this, we placed a tulip on our
bulletin board. Our expected goal was _____ tulips. We did/did not
reach this goal.

Your child received a conduct card which shows the grade earned
for_____ (behavior). When behavior was
positive, no tulips were punched on his or her conduct card. Negative
behavior resulted in one tulip being punched for each offense. Our grading
system is:

_____ — _____ "bad" tulips–satisfactory

_____ — _____ "bad" tulips–unsatisfactory

(____ total "good" tulips possible)

Please read your child's conduct
card, sign it, and return it to school
with your child tomorrow. If you
have any questions or concerns,
please call me at school at this
number:

_____.

Sincerely yours,

_____
(teacher)

110

_____
Date

Dear_____,

_____

_____

_____

_____

_____

_____

_____

_____

_____

Love,

_____

Letter
Home

Decorate your classroom with several live, blooming tulips so that children can see their structure and natural beauty. Get some tulip bulbs to display also. Invite someone from a florist shop or a horticulturist to talk to your children about flowers. Provide an opportunity for children to draw, color, or paint flowers. Display finished artwork. (Give each child a bulb to plant!)

Read Eric Carle's book *The Seed* to your class. It makes a great introduction to the study of plants. The artwork provides a great example of watercolor. The children could create their own *seed* books, written and illustrated by them! How exciting!

Go on a nature walk around your school, if possible. Look for types of flowers that grow in your area. Have children sketch them, add a little color, and organize sketchbooks of their findings. Children could add to this book at home or on trips to their favorite places in the community. Someone from the Garden Club might like an opportunity to share knowledge about flowers with your class.

CELEBRATE

GA1476

A Great Starting Lineup

Class Goal
10

Home Team Behavior
Line Up
Walk in Line

Suggestions for bulletin board titles and desired behavior:
  A Great Starting Lineup (lining up)
  Swinging into Good Behavior (any behavior)
  Team Spirit (school spirit, cooperation)
  Hometown Celebration (any behavior)
  The "A" Team (any behavior)
  From the Scoreboard (any behavior)

Suggestions for using baseball player and baseball patterns:
  Enlarge the baseball player slightly and use as a cover for a baseball
    activity booklet or to label stations in the room. (See pages 121-122
    for details.)
  Photocopy several baseballs. Use them to write "good behavior"
    messages to the children to be taken home.
  Photocopy several baseballs to use as flash cards for various content
    areas.

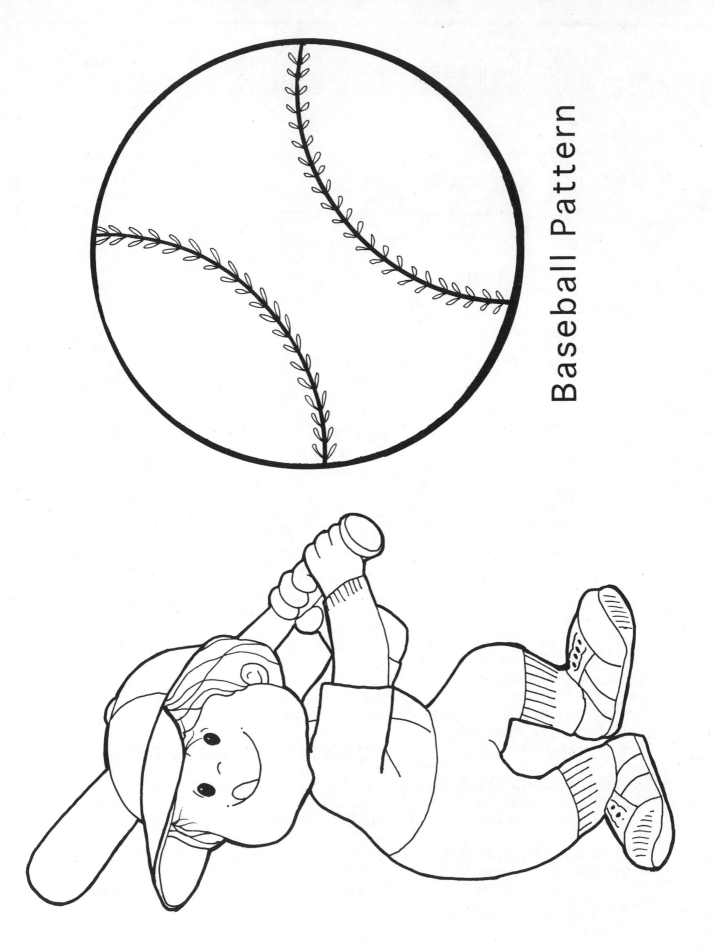

Baseball Pattern

Baseball Player Pattern

Classroom Behavior Chart

Teacher _____

Behavior _____

Week of _____

Name	M	T	W	T	F
	M	T	W	T	F
	M	T	W	T	F
	M	T	W	T	F
	M	T	W	T	F
	M	T	W	T	F
	M	T	W	T	F
	M	T	W	T	F
	M	T	W	T	F
	M	T	W	T	F
	M	T	W	T	F
	M	T	W	T	F
	M	T	W	T	F
	M	T	W	T	F
	M	T	W	T	F
	M	T	W	T	F

GA1476

Conduct Card

Child's Name _____

Date _____

Behavior

_____ Satisfactory

_____ Unsatisfactory

_____ Conference

Parent/Guardian Signature _____

116

A Message from the Teacher

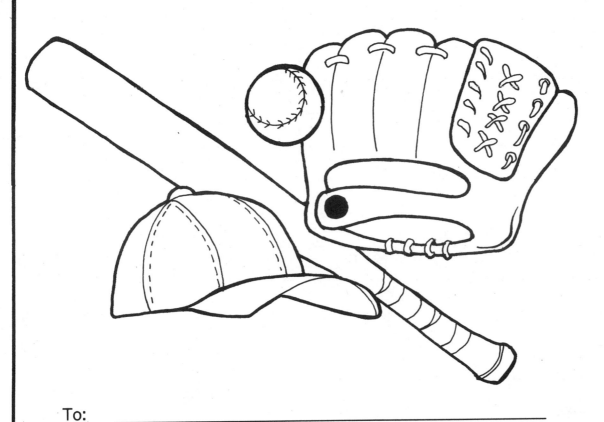

To: _____

From: _____ Date: _____

During the past_____ our class has been working on the following behavior:_____. Each day our goal was to have _____ children out of _____ show appropriate behavior in this area. When we accomplished this, we placed a baseball on our bulletin board. Our expected goal was _____ baseballs. We did/did not reach this goal.

Your child received a conduct card which shows the grade earned for_____ (behavior). When behavior was positive, no baseballs were punched on his/her conduct card. Negative behavior resulted in one baseball being punched for each offense. Our grading system is:

_____—_____ "bad" baseballs–satisfactory

_____—_____ "bad" baseballs–unsatisfactory

(_____ total "good" baseballs possible)

Please read your child's conduct card, sign it, and return it to school with your child tomorrow. If your have any questions or concerns, please call me at school at this number: _____.

Sincerely yours,

_____

A Message Comes to Me

Date _____

Dear _____,

_____
_____
_____
_____
_____
_____
_____
_____
_____
_____

Love,

_____

Letter
Home

118

Baseball Fever

Baseball fever will strike your classroom when you introduce baseball trading cards. Use the pattern on the next page and make a copy for each student in your room. Set up the ten stations listed on pages 121-122. Divide your students into teams, with three to four players on a team. The children will work at the stations as a team. The Baseball Trading Card will be an individual scorecard for station work. Have students write their names on the front, bottom part of their trading cards. (Children will be able to write their team names in the ribbon at the top and draw a picture of themselves on the front of the baseball cards when they have finished stations #1 and #6—choosing team names, team colors, etc.)

Children will receive "statistics" for station work by earning points. The point system is:

A = Home Run = 4 points
B = Triple = 3 points
C = Double = 2 points
D = Single = 1 point
E = Strikeout = 0 points

As children complete each station, they will record their scores on the backs of their trading cards in the blanks for the appropriate stations. (You can choose to grade as students complete each station or have children collect all work in the team folders and then you check them as soon as possible so that children can record their scores.

Teachers should collect all completed trading cards to record scores. You may want to choose a Most Valuable Player—an honor given to the student who scored the most home runs or had the highest point total. If you have many children who had the same scores, add bonus stations in your classroom to challenge your best "players" to score additional points.

Trading cards can be displayed on your wall in a Baseball Hall of Fame. Or you may want to create a baseball card album by buying vinyl photograph holders (5" x 7" [12.7 x 17.78 cm]) and inserting the trading cards into the plastic sleeves to display in your book. The book can be easily shared with classmates.

GA1476

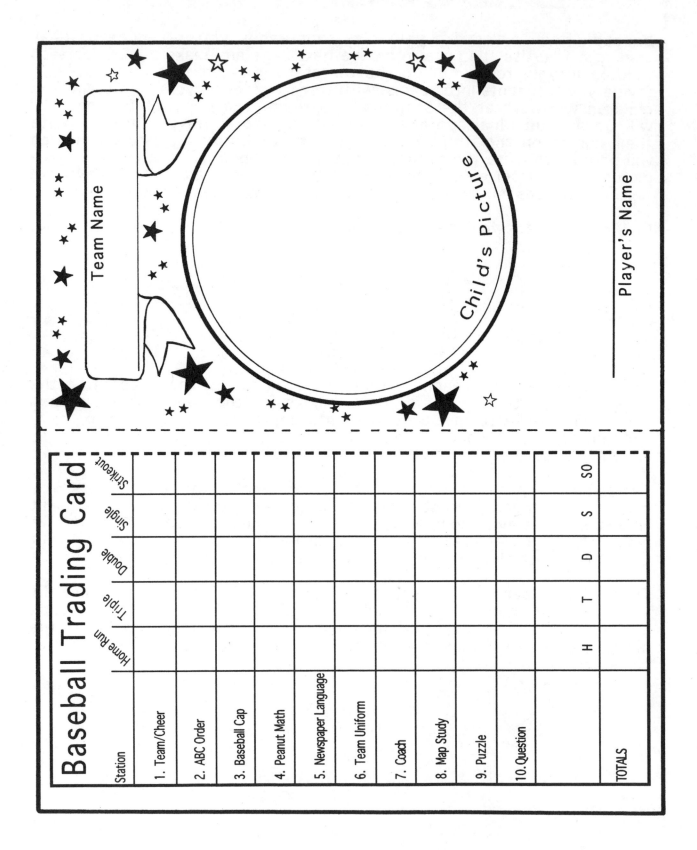

Team Name

Child's Picture

Player's Name

Baseball Trading Card

Station	Home Run	Triple	Double	Single	Strikeout
1. Team/Cheer					
2. ABC Order					
3. Baseball Cap					
4. Peanut Math					
5. Newspaper Language					
6. Team Uniform					
7. Coach					
8. Map Study					
9. Puzzle					
10. Question					
	H	T	D	S	SO
TOTALS					

Turn your classroom into fun at the ballpark! Use the little baseball player (pattern on page 114) to mark your stations. Write the station numbers on his shirt. Read through all of the ideas below to determine which ones you would like to use and prepare those suitable for your grade level. Adapt stations to suit the needs of your students and supplement with station ideas of your own.

Prior to beginning the stations, have children create their own baseball trading cards. Use the pattern on page 120 and have children record appropriate information where necessary. Display all trading cards on one of your walls or bulletin boards titled "Mr./Mrs. _____'s Baseball Hall of Fame."

Divide your class into teams of three or four students. The children will travel in these teams to the stations you set up. Each team will have its own folder in which to keep all completed work. Be sure to provide art materials or simple work sheets at the stations if you feel that your class needs them to complete the activities.

1. Have children choose a name for their team. Write it in fancy lettering. Select team colors. Choose a mascot. Write a song, cheer, or chant for the team. Be able to perform it for the class.

2. Use the baseball pattern on page 114. Write each player's name on a separate baseball. Ask children to write the names in alphabetical order neatly. (Nolan Ryan, Mark McGuire, George Brett, Bobby Bonds, Hank Aaron, Willie Mays, Roberto Clemente, Ted Williams, Mickey Mantle.)

3. See if you can buy or have donated white painter's caps for each child. (You might check a local discount store, hardware store, woodworking shop, etc.) Provide fabric paint or permanent fabric markers and have children decorate their caps with their team names, colors, mascots, etc. (T-shirts might be an alternative.)

4. Cut out several peanuts (about 4 inches [10 cm] long) from brown oaktag or construction paper. Write only one number on each peanut, beginning with 1 and continuing to 30. Ask children to choose two peanuts from the brown paper sack. Have them write the two numbers beside each other, writing "< or >" between the two numbers. (You could change the skill to addition, multiplication, etc.) Ask children to make up 25 problems.

5. Place several copies of the sports section of the newspaper at the station along with scissors and glue. Ask each team to cut out and glue on paper twenty proper nouns, common nouns, or verbs. Have them label the category they chose and glue the words below the category name.

6. Ask children to design a team uniform, complete with shirt, pants, socks, shoes, hat, helmet, banner. They must draw each article of clothing and color all items.

7. Have children pretend that they are baseball coaches. Ask them to write down ten to fifteen qualities they feel a good coach should have and tell why each quality is important.

8. Place a large map or atlas at this station. Ask children to name fifteen major league baseball teams on paper. Beside each team have them name the city in which the team is located.

9. Make up a word search or crossword puzzle using baseball words. Examples: pitcher, catcher, uniform, team, glove, baseball, bat, league, score, home run, bunt, foul, triple, double header, mound, baseline, outfield, error, etc.

10. Have one person on the team record the team's response to this question: Do you think baseball players should earn millions of dollars each year? Why or why not?

CELEBRATE

Play indoor baseball with your class. Divide the children into two teams. Put four chairs in a diamond shape in your classroom to serve as bases. Give the first player a question (spelling word, mental math problem, vocabulary word to define, etc.). If he or she answers correctly, the player walks to first base and player two sits on the chair at home plate to "bat." The game is over when either your time limit is up or when one team has reached a certain score.

It's time to autograph baseballs. Photocopy several baseballs using the pattern on page 114. Give each student a baseball. Any student who scores 100 percent on a test (or assignment) during the time period allotted may autograph baseballs of other classmates. Laminate baseballs at the end of competition so children can have them as keepsakes.

How about a 7th inning stretch! For a ten-to-fifteen-minute period during one of your classes, stop teaching and ask the children to stand by their desks. Lead them in some of your favorite exercises (jumping jacks, toe touches, arm circles, head rotations, squats, etc.). Your class will love the break!

We're on the "MOO"ve

Class Goal 5

**Behavior
In the Bathroom
On the Playground**

Suggestions for bulletin board titles and desired behavior:
  I've "Herd" You've Been Good (any behavior)
  We're on the "MOO"ve (lining up/walking in line)
  You're "Udderly" Fantastic (any behavior)
  A Taste of the Good Life (any behavior)
  Field Testing Our Behavior (any behavior)
  Welcome to the "Herd" (cooperation)

Suggestions for using cow and flower patterns:
  Photocopy several cow patterns and use them as labels for stations in your classroom.
Use part of your wall or bulletin board as a "corral."
  Photocopy several cows. When students cooperate in a positive way during any activity, write each student's name on a cow and place it in the "corral." (Use the last title above.)
Photocopy several flowers. Use them as notes home when children display positive behavior. Add flowers with their names on them to your "garden."

GA1476

Cow Pattern

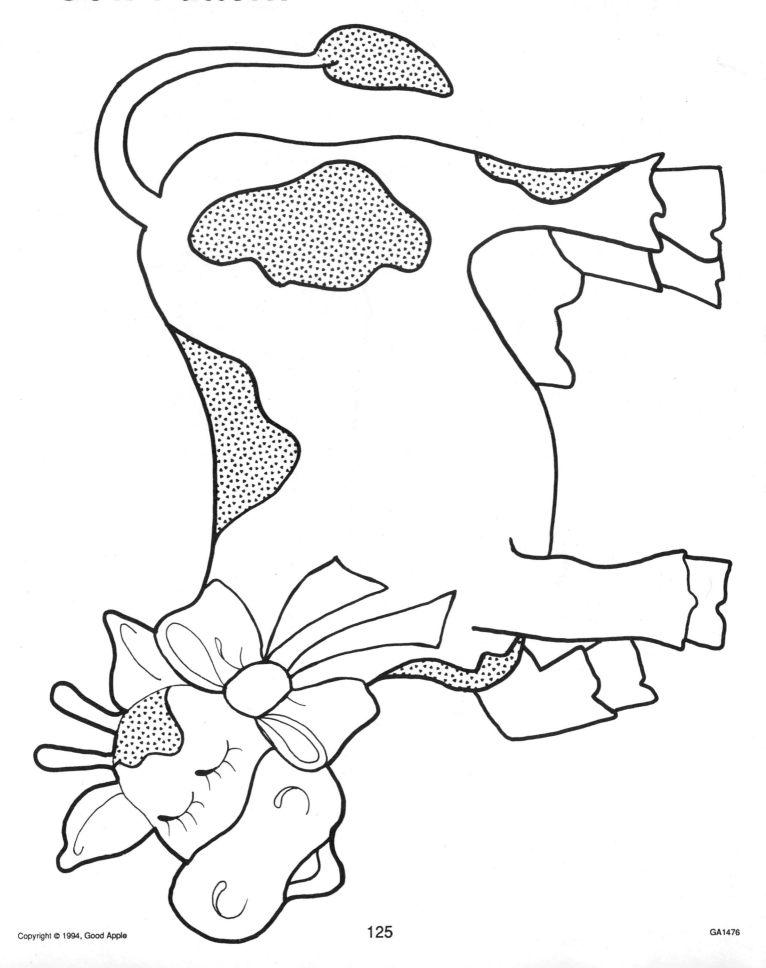

125

GA1476

Flower Pattern

126

GA1476

Classroom Behavior Chart

Teacher _____

Behavior _____

Week of _____

Name	M	T	W	T	F
	M	T	W	T	F
	M	T	W	T	F
	M	T	W	T	F
	M	T	W	T	F
	M	T	W	T	F
	M	T	W	T	F
	M	T	W	T	F
	M	T	W	T	F
	M	T	W	T	F
	M	T	W	T	F
	M	T	W	T	F
	M	T	W	T	F
	M	T	W	T	F
	M	T	W	T	F
	M	T	W	T	F

127

GA1476

Conduct Card

Child's Name

Date

Behavior _____

_____ **Satisfactory**
_____ **Unsatisfactory**
_____ **Conference**

Parent/Guardian Signature

128

GA1476

A Message from the Teacher

To: _____

From: _____ Date: _____

During the past _____ our class has been working on the following behavior: _____. Each day our goal was to have _____ children out of _____ show appropriate behavior in this area. When we accomplished this, we placed a flower on our bulletin board. Our expected goal was _____ flowers. We did/did not reach this goal.

Your child received a conduct card which shows the grade earned for _____ (behavior). When behavior was positive, no flowers were punched on his/her conduct card. Negative behavior resulted in one flower being punched for each offense. Our grading system is:

___—___ "bad" flowers—SATISFACTORY

___—___ "bad" flowers—UNSATISFACTORY

(_____ total "good" flowers possible)

Please read your child's conduct card, sign it, and return it to school with your child tomorrow. If you have any questions or concerns, please call me as soon as possible. The school phone number is

_____

Sincerely yours,

_____

Letter Home

Date _____

Dear _____

Love,
_____

Celebrate . . . "Udder"ly Great Ideas

Take a field trip to a nearby dairy. Many colleges and universities have dairy farms and would be more than happy to welcome visitors for the grand tour. If a trip to a dairy farm is not possible, perhaps a professor, county extension agent, or other knowledgeable person would like the opportunity to share with your class.

Enjoy a party of dairy delights! How about making homemade ice cream? Crank up the machine and let the enthusiasm churn. Your class will love the experience. Encourage children to bring in toppings. Borrow bowls and spoons from the school cafeteria.

Try making homemade bread and butter! Your students will love "playing" with the dough. Invite moms, dads, or grandparents in to assist. Of course take time for the grown-ups to tell stories of making homemade bread when they were little. (You might want to divide your class into three groups and have each group make something different: bread, butter, jam. What a feast! Make sure you have adult help for each group.

Divide the class into groups of four. Give each group a 3' (.91 m) piece of shelf paper on which to create a mural. You may want to assign topics for each group:
1. Draw and label dairy products.
2. Visit a dairy farm.
3. What products do we get from cows?
4. Draw and illustrate how to make homemade ice cream or butter.
5. Write and illustrate a story about a cow. Have children suggest additional topics or ideas.

GA1476

Classroom Management Notebook

Teacher: _____

School: _____

Grade: _____

Classroom Management Notebook

Table of Contents

_____ School Discipline Policy

_____ School Homework Policy

_____ School Philosophy

_____ Emergency Form for Each Student

_____ Behavior Checklist (for the Teacher)

_____ Weekly Behavior Charts (New and Used for September through May)

_____ Conduct Card Envelopes for Each Student

_____ Communication with Parents (Notes, Phone Calls, Conferences)

_____

_____

_____

_____

GA1476

Emergency Form

Child's last name _____ First name _____ Middle initial _____

Street, Route, Box _____ City _____ State _____ Zip _____

Home phone number _____ Birth date _____ Age _____

School _____ Grade _____ Teacher _____

Child's social security number _____

Transportation (A.M.) _____walker _____bus no. _____car
(P.M.) _____walker _____bus no. _____car

Legal Alert _____Explain on back.

Medical Alert _____Use back if needed.

Parent or Guardian (circle appropriate title)

Father's last name _____ First name _____ Middle initial _____

Street, Route, Box _____ City _____ State _____ Zip _____

Father's Workplace _____ Father's work number _____

Mother's last name _____ First name _____ Middle initial _____

Street, Route, Box _____ City _____ State _____ Zip _____

Mother's Workplace _____ Mother's work number _____

Parents are _____Married _____Separated _____Divorced
_____Widowed _____Single

Child lives with _____

  address _____

  phone number _____

  relationship to child _____

In case of emergency, contact _____

_____
Phone number   Relationship

134

GA1476

Behavior Checklist

Use this behavior checklist to guide you in planning and scheduling what type of behavior you will target. Take a careful look at your students to determine which skills they have mastered and which types of behavior need attention. Record the dates you practice specific behavior, add notes and comments in the space provided, and continue to assess your class. You may need to target the same behavior more than once during the school year or spend more than one week practicing that behavior. Add additional types of behavior your students need to the list provided and schedule them into your day.

Behavior	Dates Practiced	Notes
Returning materials to proper place		
Using appropriate language		
Using appropriate voice level		
Using kind words		
Talking when appropriate		
Staying in seat		
Listening to teacher		

GA1476

Behavior	Dates Practiced	Notes
Listening to others		
Cooperating with teacher		
Cooperating with others		
Being prepared for class		
Completing homework		
Completing classwork		
Staying on task		
Following written directions		
Following oral directions		
Lining up		

Behavior	Dates Practiced	Notes
Standing in line		
Walking in line		
Walking in hallway		
Keeping hands and feet to self		
Raising your hand		
Taking turns		
Being a good citizen		
Respecting own property		
Respecting property of others		

GA1476

Using Good Manners	Dates Practiced	Notes
In the cafeteria		
In the library		
During assemblies		
During fire drills		
In the bathroom		
At the water fountain		
In the hallway		
In the bus line		
On the playground		
On field trips		

Glue the form below to an envelope 6½" x 9½" (16.5 x 24.1 cm) or larger. You will need one envelope for each child in your class. Use it to collect used conduct cards. Record information on each child's envelope.

CONDUCT CARD ENVELOPE

_____
Child's name

Month	Returned	
	Yes	**No**
September		
October		
November		
December		
January		
February		
March		
April		
May		

GA1476

Communication with Parents

Name of Student	Note	Phone	Conf.	Date
1.				
2.				
3.				
4.				
5.				
6.				
7.				
8.				
9.				
10.				
11.				
12.				
13.				
14.				
15.				
16.				

140

GA1476